COGNITIVE PSYCHOLOGY

Cognitive Psychology
An Essay in Cognitive Science

George Mandler
University of California, San Diego

LEA LAWRENCE ERLBAUM ASSOCIATES, PUBLISHERS
1985 Hillsdale, New Jersey   London

Lawrence Erlbaum Associates, Inc., Publishers
365 Broadway
Hillsdale, New Jersey 07642

Library of Congress Cataloging in Publication Data
Main entry under title:

Mandler, George
  Cognitive Psychology

  Bibliography: p.
  Includes index.
  1. Cognition 2.Consciousness 3. Memory
I. Title
BF311.M227 1985   153   85-4519

ISBN Hardcover 0-89859-537-1
ISBN Paperback 0-89859-659-9

Printed in the United States of America
10 9 8 7 6 5 4 3 2 1

For Jean

Table of Contents

Preface

This book is written for the curious and for practitioners and students of the cognitive sciences. It is intended to provide an overview of a burgeoning and imperialist section of psychology--self styled as cognitive psychology. It is not a textbook. Rather it aims to provide one practitioner's view of the structure, history, and main directions of cognitive psychology. As a result it does not cover all of psychology, and not even all of cognitive psychology. However, the major trends in the field are included. More than anything else it suffers from its time-bound characteristic. Cognitive psychology, like all the cognitive sciences, is in a period of rapid change and--it is to be hoped--improvement. Thus, this is a presentation of cognitive psychology *circa* 1984.

I intend to present the broad outlines of the directions of the new cognitive psychology. As such, the book will appear to be incomplete for the psychologist reader. The major lacunae are topics that are important but outside my areas of specialization or competence or outside what I consider to be the core of cognitive psychology. These topics include psycholinguistics, neuropsychology, perception, social cognition, cognitive development, and language comprehension. The topics that are stressed, such as mentalism, memory, consciousness, are what I consider to be the core of cognitive psychology. The generality of the discipline is indicated by the excursions into fields that are not normally considered parts of cognitive psychology, such as emotion. With these goals in mind, the book provides a statement of the primary tenets, historical background, and some conceptual prejudices and biases of cognitive psychology. It could therefore be used as either overture or epilogue to the study of cognitive psychology.

For the nonpsychologist, the book stresses appropriately those areas within cognitive science that have been traditionally assigned to the psychological realm--the individual subjective realm and, in particular, consciousness. One of the expectations is that it will contribute to constructive fence building, to define the boundaries and interfaces between psychology and other cognitive sciences such as artificial intelligence, neurosciences, linguistics, and philosophy.

The occasion to write this book came at an opportune time. I had just finished the manuscript for my book on a cognitive approach to emotion and stress (MIND AND BODY, Norton, 1984), in which I explored some aspects of cognitive psychology in order to put emotion into its proper context, when Don Norman and Andrew Ortony approached me with the idea of a small book on cognitive psychology. I decided to take this opportunity to enlarge on some of the "cognitive" aspects of the emotion book, and also to add some more recent notions on consciousness and to summarize a career long interest in memorial phenomena. Soon after I started writing, it became apparent to me that this was going to be more of a personal statement than the kind of tutorial that Norman and Ortony had in mind. Eventually we agreed on that evaluation and came to a friendly parting of the ways. I am still grateful to them for providing the impetus that resulted in this book. Some of it has been developed from positions and presentations in MIND AND BODY. Other sections had their beginnings in other contexts during the past 2-3 years. My general concerns with the nature of contemporary psychology were first discussed at the American Psychological Association meeting in 1981 (Mandler, 1981b). Parts of the chapter on consciousness were presented to the Division of General Psychology at the August 1983 meeting of the American Psychological Association (see Mandler, 1983). Various comments on psychoanalysis incorporated here were presented at a Symposium on "Psychoanalysis and cognitive psychology: Convergences and divergences" at the same meeting, and some of the discussion of the cognitive sciences in Chapter 1 is adapted from my chapter on the cognitive sciences (Mandler, 1984a).

I am grateful to many people who formed my appreciation of cognitive psychology. I am indebted to my colleagues at UCSD, and particularly to Roy D'Andrade, Jean Mandler, Dave Rumelhart, and to my students over the past several years. As usual, Jean Mandler read and commented on an early draft, and William Kessen provided a friendly critique of the manuscript. Roy D'Andrade and Aaron Cicourel also commented constructively on an earlier version, and Michael Mandler and Andrew Ortony drew my attention to some infelicities. All of them are absolved of any errors of omission or commission that have persisted. I also acknowledge the research support of the National Science Foundation, which had both direct and indirect effects on the preparation of this book.

La Jolla, January 1985   George Mandler

CHAPTER 1

Origins and Relationships

PRELUDES TO MODERN COGNITIVE PSYCHOLOGY

The field of psychology in general, and experimental and theoretical psychology in particular, have been in a state of turmoil, deconstruction, or reaffirmation. Which of these diagnoses one accepts depends on one's position and investment within the field. For the cognitive psychologist, the attitude has been primarily one of reconstruction within a hazily defined tradition and deconstruction of other inherited modes of approach. I shall concentrate on the more positive views but do not want to lose sight of the possibility that this development too is transitory, in anticipation either of a new synthesis or an old despair. The concept of a "new" psychology has appeared with remarkable regularity within the field; the cycle has a periodicity of about 30 years starting circa 1880. The intent of these pages is to examine the latest of these "novelties" with some hope that it represents a truly new beginning.

The ferment in theoretical psychology that has been with us for the past quarter century has produced some agreement about an agenda for psychology, even though it has not yet produced paradigmatic agreement on the data base or specific theoretical processes. I shall return to the trends toward methodological agreements shortly, but first I want to identify some of the antecedents of contemporary cognitive psychology. The currents I want to identify are surely not the only ones, but I believe they are important in having produced the tensions that set the scene for a new synthesis.

The most obvious heritage (or cross) that marks us is the behaviorist interlude in American psychology. One of the signal characteristics of behaviorism was its rejection of theory, embodied in the rejection of mentalism. Mentalism involves the assignment of theoretical, hypothetical functions to the human - functions that determine and guide observable behavior. The rejection of theoretical mental functions can be related to a characteristic of the American puritan and fundamentalist traditions, as expressed in both functionalism and pragmatism--the objection to the abstract, the fancy, and the fictional. Behaviorism was a peculiarly American invention, although with parallels, but not identities, found in Russian psychology. I shall presently discuss the radical behaviorists' solution to the lack of theory--the abdication to physiology. With later behaviorists, the rejection of complex theory was more obscurely clothed, but it can be found in such locutions as the assignment of behavioral characteristics to the theoretical notions advanced, as in Hull's little r's and s's that were internal counterparts of external observables.[1] For a field that needed to replace physiological with mental mechanisms, the conceptually impoverished attempt at theory embodied in serially ordered S-R mechanisms, together with the avoidance of mentalistic evidence, was patently inadequate. Theories that incorporated complex dynamic processes were needed to be responsive to the new phenomena and to the wider issues that psychologists were willing to address.

The positive contribution of behaviorism that has fed into cognitive psychology can be found in its founding assertions--the critique of the equally impoverished introspectionism of Titchener.[2] Behaviorism once and for all destroyed the claims that trained introspection was the high road to the components and constituents of human mental function, or that such introspection represented the proper objective scientific method for psychology. Even the most passionate antibehaviorist cognitive psychologist today has accepted the heuristic distinction between

---

[1] For example, Hull (1951).

[2] Titchener (1898).

what is observable--and therefore serves as evidence for our theories--
and what is theoretical and inferred. The extensive and sensitive
current work on the nature and function of consciousness and on the
permissible uses of reports of private experiences are the contemporary
fruits of that development.

The antitheoretical stance of behaviorism was echoed in psychology's
neighboring disciplines. In philosophy cognitive events referred frequently to the conscious knowledge of the individual, and the affinity
between Wittgenstein's and the behaviorist position on language has
been widely noted.[3] Similar attitudes pervaded anthropology and
linguistics during the early part of the century. The avoidance of
theory also hopelessly confused the mind-body argument, though that
confusion has fueled the survival of the issue through the centuries.
Specifically the mind-body question was posed as one of the relation
between physical events and conscious mental data. This is somewhat
like asking about the mysterious relationship between the metal used in
a four cylinder engine and the speed of the car it inhabits, or between
the number and kinds of individual cells in the human kidney and its
blood cleansing function. It seems obvious that such questions can, in
principle, only be answered by reference to inferred theoretical relationships between the way engines and cells work on the one hand and the
way cars and kidneys operate on the other. In the absence of any mental theory to relate to physical theories about the brain, the relationship
remained mysterious. And the primitive materialism of the nineteenth
century further promoted the notion that the only "real" events were
the physical.

One of the historical attitudes that has marked psychology is the
belief in the theoretical priority of physiological mechanisms. That particular attitude has a respectable history and eminent defenders - William James and B.F. Skinner among them. I read the history of
psychology in part as a history of the delay in generating psychological
theory; to develop explanatory principles (that is, useful fictions) that
are wholly psychological in nature. Up until the end of the 19th century explanatory principles were sought in the physiology of the organism, and of course primarily in its neurophysiology. As long as little
was known about the nervous system, it was possible to construct
explanatory physiological fictions that seemed appropriate for psychological purposes (as did John Locke and David Hartley, for example).
By the end of the 19th century, these reductionist units had become
more palpable and James had to assign theoretical functions to "real"
physiological mechanisms. And what was "real" was the then current

---

[3] As in Wittgenstein's rather narrow and behavioristic view of the "outward criteria"
needed for "inner processes." (Wittgenstein, 1953).

state of physiological knowledge. Associative mechanisms are explained in terms of brain mechanisms, consciousness arises out of some complex action of brain centers which have the "aptitude for acquiring habits."[4] Forty years later, one of the consequences of such an approach could be found in the radical behaviorists' rejection of theoretical psychology, in part because of their insistence that the explanatory principles were more likely to be found in the physiology of the organism. For example, Skinner[5] in rejecting any conceptual, and particularly mentalistic explanatory principles, suggests that physiological explanations are most likely to "win out." The current remnants of that position are found in a view of the relation between psychology and physiology that is not just reductionist but also insists that theoretical concepts should have a physiological flavor, or--worse--that they must conform to current physiological knowledge and speculation.

An independent psychology develops its own specific and peculiar theoretical concepts and principles - it is mentalistic in the best sense. Once firmly established such a "pure" psychology will, in fact, be better able to establish the inevitable and desirable bridges to the neighboring sciences. Psychological theory that is not bound by a commitment to the language or approximations of physiological science can be instrumental in furthering the bridging theories and research that will bring about a theoretically and empirically useful integration. A rigid hierarchical approach to the relation between psychology and physiology encourages premature reductionism. It also inhibits fruitful and creative interactions between the two fields. We must be aware of physiologists' insights, as they must be of ours. The useful interaction between these two disciplines is probably more likely to be found in research that concentrates on those edges of the two fields where theory as well as empirical findings are actually in contact and where useful and justifiable extensions (in both directions) are possible. Modern (cognitive) neuropsychology is the best current example of that approach.[6] In overcoming the commitment to physiology as the theoretical (explanatory) underpinning for psychology, what was needed was a psychology that was able to substitute for the (often vague) physiological mechanisms the mental mechanisms necessary for a full theoretical analysis. Cognitive psychology is marked primarily by its exercise of that theoretical function.

---

[4] James (1890, p. 103).

[5] Skinner (1964).

[6] See, for example, Coltheart, Patterson, and Marshall (1980) and the new journal COGNITIVE NEUROPSYCHOLOGY.

The change from a theoretically limited view of mental events to a richly theoretical one needed the postulation of complex and "inaccessible" theoretical entities. That step was taken by Freud in his use of the unconscious as a theoretical device and by the Würzburgers in their assertion that there were mental determining events that had no counterparts in conscious processes (or specifically in conscious imagery).[7] These developments did not come to full fruition until cognitive psychologists had digested the lessons and mistakes of introspectionism and behaviorism. The new trends were adumbrated in the first half of the century, first in psychoanalytic theory but also in experimental psychology in the work of Selz who spoke of underlying structures and operators, by the Gestalt psychologists who introduced theoretical mechanisms that structured perception, and by some of the early cognitive psychologists.[8] All of these depended on theoretical mental structures to construct the phenomenal unity of consciousness and to account for observable consequences in human actions. Throughout this period psychologists flirted with phenomenalism and phenomenology, attempting to use the fleeting contents of consciousness as the building blocks of the science. Both the older cognitive psychologies and the more philosophically oriented ones tried to incorporate phenomenological principles in their theory and practice. They were then, as they are now, not successful, in part because phenomenological analyses often turned into verbal ones. However, the insistence and persistence of phenomenological concerns did serve as foils against behaviorism, and they are important reminders for cognitive theorists.

This brief overview of the emergence of a cognitive point of view is ethnocentric in its focus on North American developments. During that period, British psychology was relatively uninfluenced by the behaviorist upheaval and was, in contrast, concerned with problems of underlying theoretical structures. That tendency is particularly visible in the work of F.C. Bartlett whose very modern schema-based approach to problems of memory unfortunately received little attention in North America.[9] Two representatives of that tradition deserve special attention: Kenneth Craik and Donald Broadbent. Craik's work, abruptly interrupted by his premature death, addressed cognitive issues on a variety of topics and provided a new direction for British psychology. That direction is exemplified by Broadbent who has not only continued

---

[7] See Chapter 3 for a discussion of the discovery of imageless thought at the University of Würzburg in the early 20th century.

[8] Selz (1913), Frijda and deGroot (1981), Koffka (1935), Snygg and Combs (1949).

[9] See, for example, Bartlett (1932).

to be one of cognitive psychology's leading lights, but who also contributed significantly to the turmoil of the 1950s with his "Perception and communication."[10] French psychology made its major contribution to modern cognitive psychology by providing important forerunners and pace setters, such as the Swiss, but francophone, Jean Piaget, Eduard Claparède, and Alfred Binet. In recent years, French cognitive psychology has again been revitalized.[11] German psychology provided many of our ancestors such as Otto Selz and the Gestalt triumvirate of Wolfgang Köhler, Kurt Koffka, and Max Wertheimer. Again, recent years have shown a resurgence of a cognitive approach.[12]

Among all the other forerunners of a cognitive psychology, one deserves special mention: the honorable tradition of psychophysics. Experimental psychology has usually identified with the tradition of research established by Wilhelm Wundt and transplanted in a somewhat different form to North America by E.B. Titchener. From the beginning, psychophysical work, parented by G.T. Fechner and Hermann Helmholtz, diverged from the mainstream, to the point of being essentially unaffected by the behaviorist dogmas. The psychology of psychophysics was and is mathematical and nonbehavioristic, concerned with introspection, and often looking toward neurophysiology for evidence and theoretical integration. Its development, somewhat separate from the rest of psychology, has left it on a slightly different, typically more highly developed, track. Closely related to psychophysics were the developments in mathematical psychology in midcentury.[13] While stochastic and other models did not come entirely from the psychophysical tradition, psychophysics and traditional experimental psychology shared many common concerns as well as people and significantly contributed to the ideas that made cognitive psychology possible.

---

10 Craik (1943, 1966), Broadbent (1958).

11 See, for example, Le Ny (1979), Lecocq and Tiberghien (1981).

12 For example, Klix and Hoffmann (1980).

13 See, for example, Bush and Mosteller (1955).

FIVE YEARS IN THE FIFTIES

It is very rare that one can specify the beginnings of a particular movement, whether in politics or economics or in science, as precisely as we can identify the beginnings of modern cognitive psychology. The various tensions and inadequacies of psychology in the first half of the twentieth century cooperated to produce a new movement that first adopted the label of information processing and later became known as modern cognitive psychology. Most of it happened in the 5-year period between 1955 and 1960. What is particularly fascinating about that period is that major changes in attitude, method, and approach occurred more or less simultaneously in a number of different fields. These disciplines--including artificial intelligence, anthropology, cybernetics, communication theory, linguistics, and psychology--had tenuous connections with one another at the time.[14] And yet within 10 to 20 years they would be identified as the components of the newly emerging discipline of cognitive science. Cognitive science started during that 5-year period, a happening that is just beginning to become obvious to its practitioners.

The detailed history of that period is still to be written, and the social and cultural mise-en-scène, the historical reasons (in the wider sense) for the ferment of the late fifties remain to be explored. We should at least be curious about the conditions of the times that provided the context within which these common themes among diverse disciplines emerged. At the basis of my curiosity lies the belief that science is as much a product, a constituent, and a determinant of culture as are any of the more popular components of culture, such as political institutions, modes of production, religious beliefs, and personality constellations. By seeing science as culture, we can also avoid the sterile histories of science, and particularly of psychology, that are essentially litanies of "who did what and when" and sometimes "to whom." Rather than look for the keepers of the grail, we might look at the temper of the times, in keeping with Winston Churchill's reminder that events are rarely determined by extraordinary people but rather by ordinary people faced with extraordinary events.

---

[14] See Miller (1979) for a personal account, Newell and Simon (1972) and Kessel and Bevan (1985) for a general one. A more constrained account, concentrating on computer science and artificial intelligence, is presented by McCorduck (1979).

One hint of the causes of the cognitive upheaval can be found in the larger picture of industrial society. The late 1940s and early 1950s marked the appearance of the major intellectual forerunners of the change in the productive modes of Western industrial society. The transistor was invented in 1947, the integrated circuit was developed in the late 1950s, and the concept of the modern computer was explored by John von Neumann and others during those same years. These landmarks, recognized as such much later, laid the groundwork of a change in industrial society that we are in the process of observing. Western society's change to the present technological postindustrial stage was indexed by these necessary technical tools. These tools changed the intellectual climate of our sciences, just as they changed the nature of society as a whole. We observe it in the international marketplace, in labor/industry relations, and in the nature of modern warfare--and in its apparent march toward human destruction. It is no less reflected in the way we think about psychology and, in the wider sense, about human nature. The cognitive view in turn defines our attitudes about intelligence, both synthetic[15] and natural, and its "uses." Human beings are rarely seen to exercise judgment and intelligence, they are said to "use" them. People are seen to "have" predetermined skills; they are at the mercy of their biological destiny. These trends are apparent in the revival of the faculty view of psychology, i.e., people "have" different faculties, strictly separate and little affected by experience.[16] The computer in turn achieves a reified status as a thing-in-itself. Instead of people using computers, they are perceived as interacting with them. Human beings become extensions of the technological achievements. Lest the denizens of the ivory tower consider themselves exempt from the socio-cultural imperatives, consider just their metaphors as they talk of executive, control, and slave systems, of working memories and of competing activations. What is still left open is the question about the social conditions that gave rise to the technological inventions and their consequences in particular times and places.

During those 5 years of cognitive invention, new theoretical approaches were widely discussed, new questions raised, old assumptions abandoned, and new solutions proposed. It is impossible to list all the important actors, papers, and books of that half decade, or all the small and large conferences that the participants retrospectively can identify as the watershed events. Among the meetings relevant to psychology were the Minnesota Conference on Associative Processes in

---

[15] Using John Haugeland's felicitous phrase.

[16] For a philosophical reflection of that view, see Fodor (1983).

Verbal Behavior in 1955,[17] the Second Symposium on Information Theory at MIT in 1956,[18] the Gould House Conference on Verbal Behavior in 1959,[19] and the London Symposium on the Mechanisation of Thought Processes in 1958.[20] In specific areas of psychology, the ferment reached memory,[21] attention,[22] emotion,[23] perception,[24] personality theory,[25] developmental psychology[26] and many others. The important statements that bounded the new developments in psychology were the publication of Donald Hebb's integration of a "conceptual nervous system" with the first sounds of a cognitive approach at the beginning, and George Miller, Eugene Galanter, and Karl Pribram's view of the future toward the end of the initial turmoil.[27] At the institutional level, the beginning of the new decade and the maturity of cognitive psychology was marked by the opening of the Harvard Center for Cognitive Studies by Jerome Bruner and George Miller in 1960. And by the mid 1960s the "new" psychology was well established and its then current status was proclaimed by Ulric Neisser.[28]

---

[17] Jenkins (1955).

[18] For the most part published in the IRE *Transactions on Information Theory.*

[19] Cofer (1961).

[20] See *Mechanisation of Thought Processes,* (1959).

[21] Cofer (1961, reporting on a conference held in 1959); see Mandler (1967b) for a summary.

[22] Broadbent (1958), Treisman (1964).

[23] Schachter and Singer (1962).

[24] Hochberg (1968, 1981).

[25] Mischel (1968).

[26] Primarily in the rediscovery of Piaget.

[27] Hebb (1949), Miller, Galanter, and Pribram (1960).

[28] Neisser (1967).

PSYCHOLOGY AND THE OTHER COGNITIVE SCIENCES

The relative isolation of the various cognitive sciences prior to the late 1950s can be found in current echoes of the pre-50s parochialism. In discussions of the sources of the changes in the cognitive sciences during the last quarter century, credit is frequently given exclusively to one or the other of the disciplinary participants. Both linguists and artificial intelligencers like to claim parenthood of cognitive psychology; and cybernetics sometimes claims grandparenthood. For example, it is sometimes asserted that cognitive psychology was fathered by the emergence of transformational grammar in linguistics, though it can easily be documented that important trends within the psychological developments existed before the linguistic ones and certainly that some of the actors within psychology started on the cognitive path before they had even heard of the seminal work on transformational grammar.[29] Other examples of such claims of priority are found in assertions circulating within the AI community that the change in psychology came about as a result of such AI inventions as knowledge representation and control procedures. Although the notions of representation and procedure (processes) were central to the development of the cognitive sciences, and of cognitive psychology in particular, both concepts have an honorable history in prescientific psychology and in the psychology of the turn of the century.

Representation and Process

Representation and process are the primary foci of all the cognitive disciplines, and it is symptomatic of our acceptance and their importance that we rarely hear anybody question these two foundations. In fact, our acceptance of representation and process as basic to the cognitive enterprise is exemplified by the arguments that go on now about the nature of representations, about the utility of the distinction between the two concepts, and generally about the fine points of their use, not arguments about whether cognitive science should be *about* something like representation and process. We are more concerned about distinctions between analogic and propositional representations or

---

[29] These trends can be seen in the area of perception generally, as well as in memory and concept learning. See, for example, Bruner, Goodnow, and Austin (1956), Bousfield (1953), Hovland (1952), Miller (1956), Rock (1957). And an important forerunner of the general cognitive development of psychology was the "new look" approach in perception, as seen, for example, in Postman, Bruner, and McGinnies (1948).

between declarative and procedural knowledge.

Representation in the widest sense of the term is the central issue in cognitive psychology.[30] The concept of representation is intimately tied to, and possibly identical with, the issue of useful theory. Representational systems are theoretical constructs that are postulated as responsible for (that cause or generate) the observable thoughts, actions, etc. of the organism. There is of course no one-to-one correspondence between an act and its representation; we do not use the term representation in the sense of a symbol that "stands for" some other event. The representation of knowledge, in other words, is the theoretical system that is constructed in order to explain, understand, and predict the behavior of organisms. In that sense psychologists (and linguists and others as well) use representation somewhat differently from the way it is used by the artificial intelligence community. The latter are usually directly concerned with the concrete implementation of representations, whereas other cognitive scientists tend to be more interested in the representation of knowledge in principle and only as a consequence in particular representations embodied in specific implementations. But we are all talking about the same thing. Psychologists have benefited from their AI brethren's insistence on implementation, particularly as it is related to the clear statement of theory and its testability.

If we are to have any kind of reasonable theory about human thought and action, then we must have a system that represents what the organism knows. Thus, representation becomes a necessary part of any mental theory. A commitment to the importance of representation leaves open the *kind* of representational system one wishes to use or construct. The concept of deep structure, primarily introduced in linguistic theory, also addresses the issue of representation. Deep structure, as opposed to surface structure, refers to the underlying representation out of which linguistic expressions and other human products of the organism are constructed.

Representation in a narrow sense would provide only more or less static sources of cognition; we also need the processes that shape representations and transform them. Together, representation and process provide the theoretical analyses that explore the construction of experience and action. Thus, the other central concern of cognitive psychology is how thoughts and acts are produced and the specification of the processes that operate on representations. These processes include operators, search and storage mechanisms, inferential processes, and many others. Mental processes are a necessary part of knowledge and the postulation of representation and process is one convenient distinction among overlapping concepts and inextricable

---

[30] A more detailed discussion of these issues is developed in Chapter 2.

components of mental functioning.

I have deliberately oversimplified the distinction between representation and process in order to make the case for two general classes of cognitive events. In fact, of course, we talk about the representation of processes and about the possible distinction within representational systems between declarative and procedural knowledge. However, the general concern with representation is not a new one for psychologists. Wundt dealt with the representation of sentence structures, Helmholtz with the process of inference, Freud with the representation of needs and desires and with the processes that bring them to consciousness, the Gestaltists with representation of perceptual wholes and with the processes involved in the construction of percepts, and so on. It has been in the last 20 years that psychologists have become primarily concerned with these issues and have made representation and process the deliberate and central issues of psychology. But, as I have indicated, these issues are finally only symptoms of a concerted effort in psychological theory--the acceptance of and cumulative accent on the development of complex theoretical structures.

For the *artificial intelligence* community the two concepts came with their baby teeth. From the beginning, the AI business was about representation and process. AI is concerned with representing structures and knowledge and with devising processes that can operate over them. In *cognitive psychology* the invention of useful theoretical devices, both in the representation and the processing of knowledge, was a hallmark of the renaissance of the 1950s. Dynamic systems were part of psychology's heritage from the French and German psychologies of the early twentieth century, but the models were crude and their influence faded during the behaviorist interlude. In the 1950s we rediscovered and have reestablished intellectual connections with the insights of Otto Selz and the Gestaltists, with the French and Genevan schools, and with the pervasive contributions of the psychoanalytic enterprise. Mentalism, in a new form, once again became the modal approach, and the old traditions of schematic representations and the analysis of consciousness *(Bewusstseinspsychologie)* became commonplace. In *anthropology,* the late fifties saw the emergence of representational models in an area focal to anthropological thought, the investigation of terminological systems (for example, in the investigation of kinship terminology).[31] The development of transformational grammars in *linguistics* and the notion of deep structure similarly can be seen as the discovery of underlying representations and the processes that operate

---

[31] Goodenough (1956), Lounsbury (1956).

on them.[32] By now, of course, linguists of all persuasions, whether the messengers of universal truth or not, are concerned with the nature of the representations underlying language and their internecine struggles are more concerned with theories of representation than with matters of fact.

If these common concerns unite the cognitive sciences, what distinguishes them from each other? In order to understand the domain and intent of a cognitive psychology, we need to define the boundaries, however fuzzy, between it and the other cognitive sciences. A map of the cognitive sciences will have to do in the absence of a clearly defined content core to cognitive science (writ large).

The Domains of the Cognitive Sciences

Methodologies not only distinguish, but in fact divide our various disciplines. Method (in the broadest sense) is inextricably bound up with subject matter and theory, and I believe that the best way to draw distinctions among the cognitive sciences is to look at their different methods and domains. Such an examination will also lead to some insight into barriers to a real integration and a look at what an integration might imply.

I start with *artificial intelligence* in part because it is the most difficult to circumscribe but also because it may well be the focal one of the cognitive sciences. I see the potential (not yet quite realized) role of AI as extending toward all the other cognitive sciences. As keeper of the computational grail, the AI community may well turn out to be for the cognitive sciences what mathematics broadly has been for all the sciences. If mathematics is the queen of the sciences, AI could earn the mantle of the Prince of Wales of the cognitive sciences. The advent of the modern high speed computer has brought within reach the possibility of implementing and testing the kinds of complex dynamic systems that surely characterize the human mind both in its individual and social manifestations. From its beginnings, the computational riches of the new technology suggested the possibility of implementation of social and psychological theories. Furthermore, the test of implementation promises to be a useful tool for keeping social and psychological theorists honest. If their theories are so vague that their assumptions, axioms, and postulates cannot even be properly stated for possible implementation, or if their theoretical statements, once implemented, lead to internal contradictions and lacunae of indeterminacy,

---

[32] Chomsky (1956, 1957).

then the best advice would be: Back to the drawingboard! Granted that we have not reached the stage in which such precision is easily possible, or that many psychological and social theories even claim the degree of precision and prescription that is implied here, the goal can still be easily envisioned and is, in principle, attainable.

I do not want to imply that the major role of AI is to test other people's theories. Completely apart from developing the programs, algorithms, and formalisms that might be used in testing existing theoretical formulations, the AI practitioner has been and should be concerned with developing our vision of *possible* mechanisms and processes. In developing synthetic intelligences AI can open up a wide arena of formalisms that can be tested, adopted, and adapted in the mimicry of intelligent organisms and social groups that is practiced by theoretical cognitive science.

At the present time, we are moving somewhat slowly toward the goal of AI's becoming the repository of possible intelligences (if that is a proper goal). In fact, the AI community has roamed far beyond the domain that I have outlined. AI research often straddles the distinction between modeling synthetic or human intelligence, and in their (understandable) desire to distance themselves from traditional psychology, some AI practitioners have fallen into the very traps that modern psychology has painfully learned to avoid. Intuition, anecdotal examples, striking exemplars, and singular demonstrations of complex processes are poor substitutes for hard evidence. Free association in response to interesting problems may be a good way of revealing underlying motives, but it is not (and has not been in the past) a particularly edifying way of doing science. There is no doubt that the lure of what I have dubbed *phenomenocentrism* is very powerful.

Phenomenocentrism is a disease of the 19th century and particularly affects philosophers who, even when decrying common sense and belief systems, wish to use the conscious contents of minds as something explanatory rather than as something to be explained. Having abandoned ethnocentrism, which makes the experience of our particular human subgroup the measure of humanity, and having overcome anthropocentrism, which makes the human experience the cornerstone of our understanding of the world and other animals, we still are saddled with phenomenocentrism. Phenomenocentrism relies on the immediate phenomenal experience as revelatory of the structure of the mind and the world, as the basic building blocks of mental life. The attitude marks many philosophers as well as artificial intelligencers, and the symptoms of the disease appear among psychologists when they use fear and anxiety as fundamental givens (and even having computer programs with little nodes labelled as such),[33] or in talk about "immediate access" to the value and meaning of objects and events.[34] Although phenomenal experience is in part a function of universal human characteristics, it is also the result of local constraints. Firmly held beliefs, folk models of the mind and the world, and idiosyncratic histories all play their part in constructing our phenomenal experience.

Psychology--cognitive psychology--has as its theoretical task the construction of the processes that give rise to natural languages, to beliefs and feelings, and to the common categories: it must go beyond phenomenology. Our phenomenal world is immediate, obvious, and thereby very convincing. Unfortunately, we often forget that it too is constructed, that it is a complex product of our culture and personal histories. Even apparent collegial consensus about one's phenomenal world may reveal nothing more than socio/cultural commonalities and norms. The process of creation in science is dependent to a large extent on these intuitions and insights, and that context of discovery should not be confused with the harsh reality of verification. Even that reality may be blurred by the historical, social, and cultural presuppositions and norms that inform theorists, experimenters, and the objects of our study--all human beings.

These are not proscriptive warnings. Much that is new, fascinating, and important has been contributed by the AI work on modeling of human thought and action, but it would be helpful if we made the distinction between AI models that claim theoretical relevance to human intelligence and those that do not. The distinction will obviously be a fuzzy one, but it is likely to help overcome some of the misunderstandings between various camps within the cognitive sciences. None of this denies the need for a continuing interplay between artificial intelligence and substantive issues. AI methodology depends to a large extent on the recognition of the kinds of problems that human and other intelligent systems face and present. Nothing human (or synthetic) should remain alien to the cognitive sciences.

The domains of the other cognitive sciences are more easily described. They have established more or less firm frontiers, often as a result of extensive armed skirmishes with neighboring cognitive tribes. Within some of the disciplines, cognitivists are still involved in local conflicts, often trying to become dominant forces within their disciplines while the other cognitive sciences (one hopes) cheer from the sidelines. The best example of this particular scenario can be found in psychology, where cognitive psychology is well on its way to occupying

---

[33] See, for example, Izard (1977) and Bower and Cohen (1982).

[34] Zajonc (1984), Lazarus (1984).

the vacuum left by a dying behaviorism.

Cognitive psychology is often misnamed within psychology; it is frequently believed to be a psychology exclusively concerned with thought and knowledge. However, as cognitive psychologists reestablished a theory-rich discipline, their interests soon expanded into other areas, such as theories of skills and action and the analysis of emotional states. Their early concerns with the representation of knowledge and the complex processes of human thought earned them the cognitive label, but the domain engulfs all of psychology. Psychology has classically been considered to be the science of the isolated individual, whether acting and thinking alone or in groups of varying sizes. That particular distinction is breaking down as psychologists are becoming more sensitive to the fact that thought and knowledge are often best conceptualized as emerging from people-situation interactions (or better, symbioses). That particular trend has tended to blur psychological frontiers toward anthropology and sociology, while infusing new thought into the common areas shared with linguistics.

If one accepts the commonality between deep structure and underlying representations, *linguists* have been cognitive since the 1950s. Various linguistic enterprises, whether formalist or functional, have addressed the problem of theory, of the representations and processes that generate human language. Until recently they have been marked by their preoccupation with spoken language, but the discovery that sign language is similarly accessible to linguistic analyses has opened up new venues.

Together with the unifying themes of representation and process, the cognitive sciences also share a pervasive constructivist approach to the behavior of organisms. The emphasis is to develop systems and structures that can be said to construct the observable, evidential aspects of human thought and action. It is evident in the analyses of emotion and consciousness in psychology, in the linguists' approach toward a system that constructs human language, in the joint AI/psychology models of perception, and, finally, in the acceptance of the dictum that even our phenomenal world is, in the last analysis, constructed. Philosophers of kindred persuasions hear echoes of some of their own history in such talk.

There are remaining prejudices, fears, and assumptions that frequently interfere with effective interdisciplinary efforts. They are found primarily in the remnants of reductionism and in the intellectual imperialism of the individual disciplines. As long as one accepts a hierarchical notion of the sciences and an, in principle, inevitable reduction of the higher (softer) sciences to the more basic (harder) sciences, one tends to look over one's shoulder (if soft) to make sure that one's efforts are consistent with big sister, or (if hard) to make sure that little brother keeps within the boundaries of the permissible. For example, it is conceptually constricting and empirically unsound to use the current state of one's "harder" neighbor as a fixed constraint on one's own theorizing (e.g., psychology vs. linguistics or neurophysiology vs. psychology). Current fashions change in all fields, and one would not want to be left high and dry because the assumptions adopted from one's neighbors have been dropped by them. Conversely, the more "basic" sciences frequently forget to look at the conceptual achievements of their "softer" neighbors. The obvious danger here is that the more basic is supposed to explain the less basic phenomena, but the phenomena to be explained are described and defined within the language and conceptual system of another discipline. Whether or not reductionism is a mistake in principle, it is certainly a premature strategy at the present state of the art of the various cognitive sciences. Collaboration and bridge building at the boundaries is a much more satisfying and, at present, a more promising enterprise.

WHAT IS COGNITIVE PSYCHOLOGY?

Given the historical tensions that produced our current preoccupations and the general agreement that cognitive psychology is a theory-rich psychology concerned to a large extent with problems of representation and process, is there a difference between cognitive psychology and the mainstream of American psychology? If one surveys theory and practice in psychology today, the conclusion is that cognitive psychology either already is or is well on its way to becoming mainstream psychology. At the risk of alienating some friends and infuriating others, let me summarize the status of the possible noncognitive psychologies.

Behaviorism as a school has retreated to the study of lower animals, with few excursions into the human realm. What theory there is tries to make contact with cognitive constructs, though representational theory is still proscribed by operant purists. Stimulus-response theories (à la Yale/Iowa) are not more than quiescent. The behaviorist tradition is very much alive in the applied area, but here it is primarily an innovative and imaginative technology and not a theoretical enterprise.

Humanistic psychology has for years been the claimant of the theoretical crown. Unfortunately the claims have not been substantiated with principled arguments or a body of theory that makes interesting statements about human thought and action. Humanistic psychology is a collection of important statements about the role of interpersonal relations, moral values, and human growth. It continuously reminds the mainstream of theoretical psychology about some of its unfinished business, and many of us listen carefully to its warnings and alarms.

With some few notable exceptions, psychoanalytic theory has become stagnant. It has, as have all successful theoretical enterprises, succumbed to its success. It is only the historical and theoretical ignorance of many cognitive psychologists that prevents them from seeing that much of their work is consistent with and often derivative from psychoanalytic concerns. The symptoms are all around us; semantic networks, theories of forgetting, models for slips of the tongue, the construction of consciousness, are all consistent with psychoanalytic theory.[35]

There are fields of psychology that can claim respectable cognitive credentials independent of this more recent history, although they have not necessarily been characterized by theoretical unity. Much of social psychology was cognitive long before the new wave took hold, and it was the repository of underground cognitive wisdom during the behaviorist interlude. What is still missing is a theoretical framework for cognitive social psychology.

More than any other field, though, it is developmental psychology that can claim cognitive priorities, particularly as it rediscovered the contributions of Jean Piaget during the past two decades. In fact, the growth in the study of cognitive development has made developmental studies an integral part of cognitive psychology, and the rapprochement between Genevan and American cognitive psychologies is apparent in much current work.

If cognitive psychology is, or is becoming, mainstream psychology, then what is cognitive about this psychology, why the adjective? I believe that the "new" psychology is only accidentally called cognitive. Historically the concern with representation is a concern with the representation of knowledge, and hence the identification with cognition. However, the current use of representation clearly goes beyond any narrow definition of knowledge. On the other hand, there exists another tradition that identifies knowledge with conscious knowledge and in turns identifies the latter with the term cognition. The older cognitive psychologies, which were part of that tradition, have identified cognition with a psychology of "thinking." But modern cognitive psychology is not concerned exclusively, or even primarily, with conscious thought processes; rather it claims that representations and processes can be developed to fit the full range of human thought and action.

---

[35] See also Chapter 3.

Semantic confusions between cognition and thought have sometimes tended to produce a caricature of a cognitive psychology preoccupied with an inactive organism lost in thought. The very active "cognitive" efforts on the organization of action and the theoretical analysis of motor skills should do much to undo that misunderstanding.

What is not Cognitive Psychology?

What, then, does not fall within the purview of cognitive psychology? If one accepts the representation/process focus for cognitive psychology, an area is not cognitive when we have failed to find a reasonable model for the representations necessary to account for the relevant phenomena. At present, the major areas that remain opaque to such efforts are in the fields of differential, motivational, and personality psychology. But even there one can find instances of incursions, and the first theoretical skirmishes have already taken place. I find it surprising that an empirical gold mine like simple conditioning has not been tackled with innovative cognitive theories. After all, there exist more solid and replicable findings in that domain than in practically any other area of psychology.

Talking about psychology's subcultures, I must remove some misunderstandings about the human information processing approach. During the past two decades it has been, at least in the eyes of its practitioners, essentially equivalent with cognitive psychology. The misunderstanding arose because of the rather naive models used within the information processing community during its early days. There were boxes and arrows and the arrows dutifully went from box to box; the model was simple and serial--the serial box model. However, serial processes have given way to parallel processes and boxes to distributed representations and complex processing activities. To be interested in human information processing is to be concerned with the flow of information/knowledge within the organism and between it and its environment. It seems peculiar, therefore, to hear claims that some research project has shown the information processing approach to be incorrect. Such an approach cannot be "incorrect" or "correct." Information processing is a way of looking at the world, a framework for thinking, NOT a theory. For most of its practitioners it is a synonym for cognitive psychology.

A word about psychology and paradigmatic science. Some ten years ago I noted, in response to one of the many claims that cognitive psychology represented a paradigm shift in psychology, that one could hardly talk about such a shift when psychology had not yet developed any stable paradigm. I argued then that the paradigmatic crown in psychology was yet to be won but that some brand of cognitive psychology probably would have a good future claim. I believe that development is now well on its way. It may take another few decades for psychology to achieve all the criteria of a paradigmatic science, but the structure and point of view seem to be taking hold. We do seem to approach a common scientific culture. For the time being the commonalities are mainly programmatic; we still do not have a common set of accepted metatheoretical principles, and we are only beginning the work on an acceptable empirical data base. The paradigmatic crown may still have to be won, but the general looks of its wearer are becoming discernible.

What kind of theoretical synthesis is likely to emerge? The main characteristics seem to be associated with complex dynamic systems, with theoretical ideas that envisage the parallel operation of several distinct processes. What is behind us apparently is the view of people as passive systems receiving information from a fairly static environment, people whose future course of action is determined by the rewards dealt by an unexamined environment. Recent trends point to truly symbiotic models of the organism and its environment in which persons change as they change the social and physical environment in which they act and in which the situational changes in turn interact with individual action.

Criticisms of Cognitive Psychology

There are a number of criticisms of current cognitive psychology. Some are apt; others are based on misunderstandings. Prime among the latter is the confusion between cognitive psychology and the computer analogy. At the extreme is the charge that cognitive theory is so tightly wedded to computer language and computer processes that it will necessarily miss important aspects of human functioning or at least will try to fit psychological processes onto the procrustean bed of computer hardware and software. I believe that this criticism involves a misunderstanding both of the computer as a tool and of current cognitive theory. The versatility of the contemporary high speed computer is such that practically any theoretical model can be implemented on it, if the model is appropriately precise and unequivocal. In fact the possible implementation of theories on computational systems has become an important tool for keeping theorists honest. The threat of possible implementation is a useful way of forcing theorists to be precise, lest it turn out that a theory is too vague and indeterminate to be spelled out precisely for computational purposes or that its assumptions and axioms turn out to be contradictory. No current theory appears to be immune to possible computational implementation, and the computer does not by itself force one or another language.

While it is true that much of the language of cognitive theory is couched in terms borrowed from computational software, those terms themselves are not necessarily inhibiting; the still suspicious observer could, for example, substitute stimulus and response for input and output without much harm being done. On the other hand, there is an unnecessary tendency to reify the computational model, to imply that the human mind does in fact work like a computer. Reification is a danger that has bedeviled psychology throughout its history, and we must guard against the theoretical excesses that it spawns. More important, however, is that much of current cognitive theory is using terms and concepts that are independent of the computational framework. The best example is the current vogue of schema theory, which has its antecedents in developments that preceded the computer by decades, if not centuries. Moreover, there exist some theoretical notions that seem to be opaque to contemporary computational methods.[36]

The computer metaphor was unavoidable; it was forced by the culture of the 1950s and 1960s, just as the clockwork/waterworks metaphor was forced on Descartes by the culture of the early 17th century. Philosophy had moved away from the Cartesian metaphor by the end of the 17th century and we have moved away from the computer metaphor. The locutions that I and others use to describe the information processing flow is probably as much determined by Cartesian remnants as by von Neumannian ones. But I don't speak "computer" when I and others discuss the construction of emotion and consciousness. Cognitive psychology (or its synonym, human information processing) is a new psychology because it is theory rich, compared with theory-poor behaviorism. The computer metaphor was a useful step in the direction of novel and cumulative theory.

---

[36] See, for example, the topological considerations presented by Chen (1982).

Finally there is the most serious criticism of them all, the accusation of professional dilettantism. Psychologists in every corner of the empirical domain of psychology seem to be in search of quaint minitheories. Multiplying the psychologists by empirical subfields threatens to yield a wealth of theories well in excess of the available data. But, before such an avalanche threatens to bury us, we must be seriously concerned with the theoretical pluralism that seems to be the cultural norm. It is, of course, one of the reasons why talk about a paradigm is premature. Worse yet, these minitheories are seldom put to the test against other competing claimants; they rarely attain the age of consent to be tested. Such a development of noncumulative minitheoretical forays seems to be at odds with another impression, namely, that the psychological enterprise has become cumulative. In some fields, memory and attention, for example, the basic phenomena to be explained seem to be generally accepted and, to a large extent, their acceptance continues independent of the various minitheories advanced to explain them.

One might argue that this plethora of theoretical inventions is a youthful sign of enthusiasm, that the liberation to invent has given rise to adolescent excesses. Personally, I tend toward some such explanation. If there is a search for some common scientific culture, for a paradigm, then it is not surprising that the marketplace of ideas is filled with wares of varying quality and attractiveness. At the same time, the grand themes of representation, process, schema theory, context-dependent structures, and others are being developed within and across the busy minitheorists; there may be a forest despite all the trees. I do agree, however, that care must be taken not to create an atmosphere that encourages and rewards theoretical dilettantism, otherwise the criticisms from the precognitive establishment may turn out to be well founded. The critics ask whether the ready availability of explanations for whatever data appear on the horizon is not an advanced case of hand waving and empty theoretical jargon. These criticisms come primarily from members of an experimental establishment that used to concern itself with the proper design of experiments at the expense of theoretical relevance; they may exhibit an unfortunate bias, but often their questions are painfully to the point.

I leave my quest for cognitive psychology with the same questions with which I started: What is the cultural/historical context that has generated this new busy-ness? I do not ask for the philosophical assumptions behind contemporary cognitive psychology, because the philosophies too are the children of the culture, but I do want to pose for philosophers and historians of psychology the question about the deep structure of our theory and of our metatheory. What are the cultural and social imperatives to which we respond when we do cognitive

There is a sense in which we are likely to remain blind to the cultural imperatives that shape our thoughts and actions. The past experience of historical analysis suggests that it is only in succeeding generations that we are able to discern the themes that directed previous epochs. Behaviorism seems to have been an expression of some of the most pervasive themes of American culture of the nineteenth century and of the zenith of American capitalism. Cognitive psychology is more transcultural, not identifiable with any particular national experience. Cognitive psychology also seems to be more sensitive to the necessity of incorporating other theoretical systems, to listen to the achievement of other, and prior, endeavors, and to establish enduring links with its neighboring cognitive sciences.

But I did not intend to end these remarks on a purely speculative note. Whatever the future of theoretical psychology, for the time being cognitive psychology is alive and well, quite young and sprightly, sometimes marked by adolescent enthusiasm and excesses. It will be fun watching the next few decades.

METHOD AND PSYCHOLOGY

The single characteristic that differentiates cognitive psychology from other cognitive sciences such as artificial intelligence, anthropology, and linguistics is its commitment to experimentation and the use of controlled evidence. For better or for worse, psychology adopted or inherited the experimental method of the natural sciences. Theories, models, and hypotheses were often seen merely as vehicles for the generation of experiments. Although that may be seen as a perversion of both theory and experimental techniques, it generated the emphasis on the design of experiments and detailed statistical analyses. The plethora of such techniques and their experimental competences did make psychologists highly sensitive to theoretical claims that either were not subjected to empirical tests or were opaque to such tests.

From one point of view, experiments are decision methods; they are designed to settle disputes over alternative explanations of phenomena. This does not claim that the *experimentum crucis* is either a frequent occurrence or even a defensible concept. Rather, experiments provide some of the relevant phenomena for and constraints on possible explanatory (theoretical) constructions. When we are lucky, it makes possible new insights by challenging our theoretical prowess with unexpected results or unpredicted findings. From that vantage point, experiments provide a way of producing interesting phenomena. Experiments are a useful antidote for two tendencies: the proliferation of theoretical speculation on the one hand and rationalist approaches on the other. Theoretical proliferation often occurs when a particular theory or model is initially highly successful. Subsequent aficionados of the theory are then tempted to play with the internal structure of the theory, with extensions and elaborations, and tend to engender a lack of concern for the relevant evidence. One example can be found in the psychoanalytic literature. Rationalist or formalist arguments for psychology are not unrelated to internal analyses of theoretical structures for their own sake. Formalists (often tied to linguistic theories such as Noam Chomsky's) rely much more heavily on axiomatic methods, starting with plausible (often phenomenally rational) assumptions about the relevant domain. Their approach is then concerned with the internal structure of such a system. Their criteria are more often parsimony and elegance than evidence obtained from reliable observation. The distinction between formalists and functionalists (which is a widely used description of the "other" camp) is not an all-or-none divide; it tends to describe preferences rather than absolutes. Functionalists (and most psychologists) tend to be concerned with specific mechanisms in the cognitive arena, building up the theoretical structure needed to understand the (experimentally) observed performance of the system (the human being) under study. Rationalist and formalist theorists tend to argue from first principles. To say that both kinds of approaches are needed for a fruitful understanding of intelligent systems does not eliminate the distinction or the arguments between the two groups. To accuse functionalists of lacking a principled approach or of being seduced by piecemeal observation or to consider formalists as working at a level of abstraction that is far removed from "true" structure of the human mind is not particularly productive. However, one can argue that this kind of tension may in fact be useful in providing appropriate foils for the two respective groups.

The argument between formalists and functionalists can be found even in a paradigmatic science like physics that has institutionalized the distinction between theorists and experimentalists. Nancy Cartwright has provided an elegant presentation of the case for an empiricist anti-formalist physical science.[37] Some of her remarks are relevant to the present argument. She argues for theoretical entities and "local" laws, but against the covering unifying laws of basic theory. The manipulation of specific theoretical entities in the laboratory justifies their acceptance. In contrast, fundamental *laws* "do not govern objects in reality; they govern only objects in models." It is the controlled experiment that permits us legitimately to infer causes. Experiments permit us "to isolate true causes and to eliminate false starts."

---

37 Cartwright (1983).

Finally, cognitive psychologists have moved significantly beyond the control/experimental group designs that dominated psychology up to the 1960s. With better control over the phenomena that we study, large-scale designs with large numbers of subjects have also declined. Cognitive psychologists seem to have learned both from psychophysics and radical behaviorism that single subject studies can be highly productive. The change in experimental approaches, together with a subordination of experiment to theory, may also be diagnostic of increasing maturity in psychology. However, little has changed the psychologist's basic commitment to experimental evidence and its interplay with theory. We have, fortunately, become more receptive to the evidence of our daily experience, and cognitive psychologists have used such evidence as a useful starting point for their investigations. But an openness to anecdotal hints has not replaced principled, controlled (and frequently experimental) observation and evidence.

CHAPTER 2

The Structure and Function of Mind

AN INTERPRETATION OF MIND

Psychologists have long understood that it is futile to try to use the common language as a vehicle for scientific abstractions and generalizations or to explicate psychology by trying to define what common concepts such as emotion or intelligence *really* are. Given that sophistication, it is surprising that many psychologists (and certainly the philosophically inclined ones) are still trying to determine what mind *is*. In the common understanding, "mind" has a variety of referents, as shown in such expressions as "I can't keep my mind on it," "I am going out of my mind," "She has a fine mind," "It is a matter of mind over body." Just this small sample seems to refer to such other events or concepts as attentional capacity, rationality, intelligence, and the influence of some noncorporeal entity. The same kind of confusion exists *pari passu* with the term "mental." At the same time, the folk models of mind deserve attention in their own right, inasmuch as they determine to some extent the way in which people consider their own and other thought processes and construct their view of the world. In any case, "mind" and "mental" are clearly theoretical terms--they are not directly observable, they are inferred from observations. And they are used freely to refer both to the self and to others. So much for the cottage industry that has grown up in philosophy over arguments concerning the existence of minds other than ones own. They are all inferred; and the remaining question is merely whether the inference is based on the observation of the self or of others.

There is a sense in which the term "mind" has been used that is highly restrictive and could provide some consensus. It uses the conscious contents as the referent for mind, including such events as conscious thought, perception, and feelings. However, for a psychologist that usage is usually too restrictive and, in any case, is better discussed within the context of the relationship between mind and consciousness.

MINDS AND BODIES

If we do not wish to restrict "mind" to conscious contents and processes, the remaining general sense appears to refer to an agency that is responsible for (determines) human thought and action. We can be all inclusive and accommodate most common language usage by using "mind" to refer to the inferred mechanisms and processes assigned to the active human being--processes that construct the contents of consciousness, determine our feelings, attitudes and beliefs, and guide our intelligent (and not so intelligent) actions. What is the relationship of such a "mind" to the physical substrate in which it operates? We are back to the mind-body problem introduced in Chapter 1 as a question about the relation between mental and physical (physiological) mechanisms. As I suggested there, the mind-body question can be posed as one concerning the relation between physical data and mental data. This requires a mental theory to be related to physical theories about the brain.

There are specific, and sometimes very precise, concepts associated with the function of larger units such as organs, organisms, and machines, concepts that cannot without loss of meaning be reduced to the constituent processes of the larger units. The speed of a car, the conserving function of the liver, and the notion of a noun phrase are not reducible to internal-combustion engines, liver cells, or neurons. Emergence is a label that has often been applied to new properties of larger assemblies. But rather than saying that the new properties emerge, it might be more parsimonious to insist that different entities have different functions. The mind has functions that are different from those of the central nervous system, just as societies function in ways that cannot be reduced to the function of individual minds. This is, of course, true even within bounded scientific fields; even physics cannot be reduced to physics, as in the case of the relation between mechanics and nuclear physics.

Much of the difficulty that has been generated by the mind-body distinction stems from the failure to consider the relation between well-developed mental and physical theories. Typically, mind and body are discussed in terms of ordinary-language definitions of one or the other. Because these descriptions are far from being well-developed theoretical systems, it is doubtful whether the problems of mind and body as developed by the philosophers are directly relevant to the scientific distinction between mental and physical systems.

Once it is agreed that the scientific mind-body problem concerns the relation between two sets of theories, the enterprise becomes theoretical and empirical, not metaphysical.[1] If, however, we restrict our discussion of the mind-body problem to the often vague and frequently contradictory speculations of ordinary language, then, as centuries of philosophical literature have shown, the morass is unavoidable and bottomless.

For example, we could, in the ordinary-language sense, ask how it is that physical systems can have "feelings." Such questions assume that we know the exact nature of the physical system and, more important, the structure of a mental system that produces "feelings." Usually, however, the question is phrased as if "feelings" were a basic characteristic of the mental system instead of one of its products. The report of a feeling is a complex outcome of the kind of mental system that will be espoused here. Not only is the experience of a feeling a product, but its expression, through a language system, is the result of complex mental structures that intervene between its occurrence in consciousness and its expression in language.[2] Thus, any question about the relation of feelings to physical systems turns out to be at least premature if we agree that feelings, however defined, are the products of a complex mental system and that the "physical" observations are products of a similarly complex physiological system. But then the question about the relation (the correspondences) between physical systems and feelings requires that we know what the physical theory and

---

[1] Mandler and Kessen (1959), Mandler (1969).

[2] The construction of "feelings" in particular demonstrates that the product is in part a function of complex cultural and social conditions incorporated into the constructive process. For an example of such cultural differences in the reaction to pain, see Zborowski (1969).

the mental theory are about and that these are unequivocal in their prediction and specified in great detail as to their structure. Until these goals are achieved, scientific questions about the mind-body problem are premature and irrelevant.

In short, there exists no special mind-body problem. It is one of many examples in which the interface between systems of explanation, theory, and conceptualization requires bridging concepts, acceptance of discontinuities, or admissions of ignorance. With the development of the explanatory systems that abut such an interface, the nature of the problem changes to the extent that, in some cases, reduction (explanation) of one system in terms of the other may become partially or even wholly possible. The mind-body problem has been the subject of special attention because it is of immediate phenomenal relevance to an active, cogitating, theory-building organism--the human being.

The emotional domain in particular has been the battleground for mind-body debates. In the seventeenth-century René Descartes made popular the question how the soul could affect the body and ideas cause actions. Except for anthropocentric and theological concerns, Descartes had implicitly supplied the answer when he claimed that, for lower animals, machines could be designed that would be indistinguishable from the "real thing." His test for the adequacy of such machines in the age of clockworks was the forerunner of a similar test that the mathematician Alan Turing developed for the age of computers. Turing's test is similar to Descartes' implied answer for lower animals: if we can design machines that think (aloud) and act like humans with ideas (minds, souls) and bodies, then we will have moved closer to solving the ancient conundrum. When a machine becomes indistinguishable from a human actor, it will represent a reasonable approximation of how humans work. In the meantime, both ideas and actions are the products of underlying representations and processes. The theory of the mind will have mechanisms that produce ideas and actions in a fashion that will give the obvious and inescapable impression that ideas cause actions. When a machine announces that it "intends to raise its third articulated limb" and, if at some reasonable time thereafter that limb in fact rises, the appearance of some "intention-thought-action" sequence will be conveyed. Any reasonable knowledge of the mechanisms will reveal the sequence of underlying processes that produce all three of the components of that sequence. Even the intention to raise the limb (or the intention to announce the intention) will be identifiable in terms of underlying processes.

This line of argument restates my more general exposition of the mind-body problem. We shall understand this "interaction" when we understand the several representations and processes and the linking processes that lead from one to the other.

REPRESENTATION AND PROCESS

The current strategy in cognitive psychology is to use representation and process as the central metatheoretical categories. I have suggested that no clear distinctions can be made between these two categories, the most obvious case being the bifurcation between declarative and procedural representations, both of which imply specific processes. The former generally implies consciously available knowledge about the world, whereas the latter typically applies to actions and procedures that are not available to conscious constructions. I return later to the distinction between these two kinds of processes when I discuss the distinction between automatic and conscious action mechanisms. Whatever such distinctions should produce, all actions and thoughts require some underlying representation, some theoretical structure that constructs and produces the observable aspects of human thought and actions. In what follows I briefly discuss some varieties of representations. An excellent discussion of the representation problem in general has been prepared by David Rumelhart and Donald Norman,[3] and a discussion of the sources and types of representation with special references to cognitive development has been presented by Jean Mandler.[4]

Central to the notion of representation is the intent that mental representations are about meaning and knowledge. Arguments about representation--what kind of systems, how many of them, how different--are essentially arguments about the nature of meaning and knowledge. I have already indicated my dissatisfaction with any kind of scientific enterprise that aims at the exhaustive definition or explication of common or natural language concepts, other than to use such devices as important starting points for the enterprise. That same argument applies to concepts such as meaning and knowledge, just as it does to memory or emotion or intelligence. Thus, arguments about different kinds of representations become either arguments about the "proper" representation of meaning and knowledge or internal arguments about formalisms, elegance, parsimony, etc. From that

---

[3] Rumelhart and Norman (in press).

[4] J.M. Mandler (1983, 1984a).

point of view, representation is not a novel enterprise; it is the old problem of finding serviceable and useful theories directed toward problems of meaning and knowledge--the primary concerns of cognitive psychologists. As a result it is often misleading to speak as if mental representations are modeling some represented "world." Representations certainly do often reflect certain worldly characteristics, but they surely serve as more than an internal model of an external world. Representations in the wider sense are theoretical devices that make it possible for the theorist to generate consequences that have some general relation to the rather vague common sense notions of meaning and knowledge. What requirements can one put on such a theoretical system? Just as in most theories, a representational system should specify the following characteristics:[5]

1. Its domain of evidence,
2. The characteristics (e.g., structure and notation) of the theoretical system,
3. The aspects of the domain that are relevant to the representations,
4. The aspects of the theoretical system that are relevant to the domain,
5. Rules for relating the theory to the evidence.

Which particular representational system will be most useful depends on such specifications and how well they fit the specific situation in which they are employed. As a result, the range of domain and specificity of representational systems varies widely. Representational systems may model narrowly as in specific knowledge domains or in human visual imagery,[6] or be more ambitious as in generalized semantic networks or in schema theory.[7] Research and theory on memory has tended toward systems that have propositional elements as their primitives, including several semantic network systems and the influential

---

[5] These characteristics are paraphrases of Steven Palmer's insightful discussion of representation (1978). However, I have replaced his "represented world" by domain and evidence, and his "representing world" by theoretical systems.

[6] For example, Bobrow and Winograd (1977) and Kosslyn (1980) respectively.

[7] For example, Norman and Rumelhart (1975) and Rumelhart and Ortony (1978) respectively.

propositional systems of John Anderson and Walter Kintsch.[8] The restriction of semantic networks to propositional ("semantic") representations has reduced their popularity and has helped the increasing popularity of general schema theories, about which more later. One influential non-propositional model has been John Morton's logogen theory.[9] The basic unit or logogen defines the information that it will accept and the responses it makes possible. The logogen is a signal detector that gathers relevant information, regardless of its sources, and, once a threshhold of activation is reached, its output is passed to response buffers and semantic systems. The model has recently been modified to incorporate modality specific categorization systems.[10]

The representation of *process* has frequently been accomplished within a general representational system, although it is also often seen as a separate class of theoretical mechanisms operating *on* representations. For example, within schema theory, processes are part of the operation of a schema that "seeks" relevant information, activates other schemas, and constrains competing schemas. On the other hand, in production systems processes are clearly separate entities. Both semantic networks and schema theoretical representations can have procedures or processes that are embedded within the more general representational system. For example, in active network structures[11] the semantic structures carry out matching processes and can build relevant new networks. Some schematic structures[12] have been designed specifically to identify relevant information, fill in missing data, and activate other schemas.

Representations that have separate processing structures use the latter to operate directly on informational structures, creating new structures, activating other processes, or lead directly to action.[13] One example is the cognitive algebra developed by Norman Anderson, who is concerned with the computational problem of weighting and combining person and object characteristics in the process of making affective

---

[8] J.R. Anderson (1976), Kintsch (1977).

[9] Morton (1969).

[10] Clarke and Morton (1983).

[11] Norman and Rumelhart (1975).

[12] McClelland and Rumelhart (1981).

[13] For an early example see Selfridge (1959).

and evaluative judgments.[14] The most influential current use of separate processes is found in production systems.[15] These systems set a problem or goal and then examine the available evidence for particular sets of data that are appropriate or relevant to these goals. When a match is found, IF-THEN statements are invoked that represent the processes that operate on the available data. Production systems incorporate some of the best lessons to be learned from stimulus-response psychology, not the least of which is their potential ability to learn new productions (associations).

The newest and most promising arrivals in the representational fold are distributed systems. Rather than data being stored in specified locations, information is distributed across the representational system.[16] Consider a set of features (f_1 to f_n) that represents all possible features or attributes of a particular event. Different mental events will be represented by different combinations of these same features, and different aspects of a representation will make use of different subsets of the sets of features. For example, a subset of these features (f_1 to f_m) may be relevant to the perceptual (visual, acoustic, etc.) aspects of the event, with the remaining features (f_{m+1} to f_n) dealing with conceptual, semantic, and related features of the event. Whenever a particular subset of these features is activated by evidence from the external world, these features will tend to activate each other on subsequent occasions when some of them occur in some future event. Thus, any presentation of an event that is similar to an existing representation (i.e., shares a number of features with it) will tend to produce activation of the entire representation, as well as greater interactive probabilities among the features on subsequent occasions. This process has been referred to as integration (see later and Chapter 4). For example, prior exposure to the perceptual features of an event leads to the integration of that set of perceptual features. Integration of the perceptual features is related to the probability that some of these features, once activated, will preferentially activate other perceptual features of the event.

---

[14] N.H. Anderson (1981).

[15] See Newell (1973), J.R. Anderson (1982).

[16] Originally, these systems were called neural models, though that usage has declined (Hinton and Anderson, 1981). For extensive discussions and applications of these models, see Rumelhart and McClelland (1985) and McClelland and Rumelhart (1985).

This kind of representation can be alternately mapped into the notion of a schema of the perceptual features, with integration developing the increasing boundedness, distinctiveness, and internal activation of the perceptual features that make up the schema. Since the representation of any single event is distributed across the system (i.e., wherever its features or attributes appear) the system is very robust. It also has the advantage of not being free of errors, i.e., it is representative of human performance. Distributed systems also automatically engage in assimilation, by incorporating partially presented information into known structures. Recent developments have shown how these distributed systems can "learn," i.e., create new structures and new knowledge.[17] Finally, a distributed representation of schemas discourages a view of schemas as fixed (often spatially fixed) and rather rigid permanent denizens of a mental system. Under a distributional view, schemas do not "exist" in the absence of relevant activation (either from the world or in a top-down fashion). Each specific experience that is relevant to a particular schemas will construct a specific variant of the schematic representation. To the extent that each experience is different from every other one, such a construction will have both unique and general characteristics. It will be unique with regard to its own particular concatenation of features and attributes, and it will be general to the extent that it activates previous correlations of features and attributes (and thereby benefits or suffers from the effects of previous experiences). In addition, each such instantiation will in turn tend to reset the values of schematic variables and have its own effect on subsequent evocations of the schema(s).

This survey of the most visible of current representational systems should convey the sense of theoretical gestation and turmoil that is currently explicit in cognitive psychology. In the end, it may turn out that no single representational system will win out, but rather that different situations, tasks, and contexts will require different representation to do full justice to the complexity of human thought. I now turn to a more detailed presentation of schema theory, partly because of its popularity and partly because of my own preoccupation with it.

---

[17] Ackley, Hinton, and Sejnowski (1985).

Schemas as Representational Systems

I use the term "schema" to conform with current usage and also to evoke similarities with Bartlett's and Piaget's usage.[18] The concept of the schema goes back at least to Kant, who viewed schemas as directing our experience. Thus, the schema of a dog is a mental pattern that "can delineate the figure of a four-footed animal in a general manner, without any limitation to any single determinate figure as experience, or any possible image that I can represent *in concreto,* actually presents."[19] Schemas are cognitive structures, which is the more general term used for underlying representations in cognitive systems. Other cognitive structures that have been distinguished from the large class of schemas are such devices as logical devices, syntactic structures, and strictly procedural mechanisms. Schemas are used primarily to organize experience, and in that role they overlap with some aspects of concepts like "plans" and "images." In current usage, other cognate concepts are those of scripts[20] and frames.[21]

Schemas are built up in the course of interaction with the environment. They are available at increasing levels of generality and abstraction. Thus, schemas may represent organized experience ranging from discrete features to general categories. For example, one schema may represent a horse's head, and another one facilitates the perception of a particular animal as a horse because of the concatenation of certain features (variables of a schema) such as a head, a tail, a mane, a certain size, a range of colors etc. That same horse is categorized as an animal because of the occurrence of certain defining characteristics or because it fits some prototypical schema.

A schema is a category of mental structures that stores and organizes past experience and guides our subsequent perception and experience. This conception embraces Piaget's invention of the schema as structuring our experience and being structured by it. The schema that is developed as a result of prior experiences with a particular kind of event is not a carbon copy of that event; schemas are abstract represen-

---

[18] Bartlett (1932), Piaget (1953).

[19] Kant (1781).

[20] Schank and Abelson (1977).

[21] Minsky (1975).

tations of environmental regularities.[22]

Schemas vary from the most concrete to the most abstract; they organize the perceptual elements of an event, as well as its "meaning" or gist. We postulate a schema for a particular object, like a chair or a specific lecture, and also for furniture and for typical lecturing behavior. We comprehend events in terms of the schemas they activate, though we have different ways of talking about different kinds of comprehension, such as perceiving, understanding, or remembering.

A schema is, in one sense, a bounded, distinct, and unitary representation. Activation of parts of a schema implies the activation of the whole, distinct from other structures and other schemas. In the activation process, partial activation of (some of) the features of a particular schema will result in the others being "filled in". In general, it is prior co-occurrence that determines mutual activation of features in the underlying representation. Finally, it should be noted that generic schemas have modal (or even canonic) values of variables. This property is related to the notion of schematic prototypes[23] which serve as reference schemas for categories.

Schemas operate interactively, i.e., input from the environment is coded selectively in keeping with the schemas currently operating, while that input also selects relevant schemas.[24] Whenever some event in the environment produces "data" for the schematic analysis, the activation process proceeds automatically (and interactively) to related schemas. When the particular knowledge domain is hierarchically organized, we assume that some activation spreads to the highest (most abstract) relevant schemas. A chair activates not only the "chair schema" but also the more general schemas such as "furniture" and possibly "things to sit on". At the same time, the activation of a schema also involves the inhibition of other competing schemas. Evidence from the environment activates potential schemas, and active schemas produce an increased readiness for certain evidence and decreased readiness (inhibition) for other evidence. The inhibitory mechanism makes it possible to access specific schematic representations without interference from

---

[22] For example, Franks and Bransford (1971). See Rumelhart and Ortony (1978) for some of the specifications of schemas, and J.M. Mandler (1983, 1984b) for a general discussion and for the use of schemas in understanding stories, events, and scenes.

[23] See Rosch and Mervis (1975), Rosch (1978).

[24] See McClelland and Rumelhart (1981), Marcel (1983b).

highly similar ones.[25]

The particular interaction between the contextual environmental evidence and the individual's available schemas accounts for both external and internal (mental) effects on perception and memory. The prior activation of schemas, determined by where we are, what we have been doing, and what we expect will focus perception and conception on specific hypothesis about likely occurrences and will favor the mental construction of plausible objects and events out of the available external evidence.

Activation processes occur automatically and without awareness on the part of the perceiver/comprehender. I return to this issue in Chapters 3 and 4. However, a distinction can be made about the kinds of activation that may occur. Activation of a schema may, under the proper circumstances, involve the target schema alone without any other mental contents being involved. In particular, these "other mental contents" may be other representations evoked by external events. For example, "rote" repetitions may typically focus on the target event (sentence or poem) without invoking any relations to its meaning (i.e., relation to other objects or events).[26] Whenever a representation is activated, whether in conjunction with other schemas or not, that activation produces *integration* of the structure. One of the consequences of the activation of the constituent features or attributes of a schema is that spread of activation within the schema not only will produce greater activation of all of its features, but also will make such mutual activations of the features of that schema more likely on subsequent occasions. As a result, the schema becomes better bounded and defined and will be a more effective unit on subsequent occasions. In contrast, a specific schema may, under certain circumstances, be activated in relation to other objects and events. This kind of activation produces *elaboration,* the relation of mental contents to each other. Elaboration is of particular importance in acquiring new knowledge structures, and becomes central in laying down memorial traces for future retrieval (see Chapter 4).

---

[25] See Rumelhart and McClelland (1982) for an implementation of this notion for word recognition.

[26] Mandler (1979a).

WORLD AND MIND: DIFFERENT STRUCTURES

Both the physical world and the mind are structured. In dealing with our surrounds, the mental system represents the structures of the world, but not in a one-to-one correspondence. This distinction is important to an understanding of the way we act and think in the world, and also for the way we build mental models of that world.[27]

The importance of that distinction is best illustrated if we reconsider the distinction between competence and performance that was so readily accepted by many psychologists, particularly psycholinguists. The distinction had its origin in the work of the French structuralists, who introduced the modern concern with the structure of human functions and artifacts. In turn, the structure of language, the basic language code, is taken to speak to the language competence of the individual, which reflects the structure of language as such, independent of the experience of the individual. Performance is, in contrast, the actual language usage of the individual, limited by experience and by cognitive and psychological factors. At times, competence has been related to language comprehension, whereas performance is seen to reflect language production. Psychologists in general prefer to see comprehension as one kind of skill and production as another, related one. The point of interest here concerns the nature of the representation that produces competence: Is it a structure that is isomorphic with the structure of the language as such?

Under one interpretation, competence refers to the underlying structure of a particular ability, skill, or characteristic, whereas performance indexes the actual instantiations and realization of that structure in human thought and action. Psychologists may have been particularly intrigued by the concept, in part because it has some analogic similarity to the learning/performance distinction that was so artfully used by the learning theorists of the 1940s. The latter placed its primary distinction on the difference between observables and representations, between data and theory. What an organism had learned and what was actually observed in behavior depended on particular situational and individual factors at the time of performance.

---

[27] See, for example, Gentner and Stevens (1982).

The competence/performance distinction is frequently a distinction between a formalist description of a system in the language of one discipline (philosophy and linguistics) and the imputed "use" of that system by a psychological entity, e.g., the human mind. In other words, competence tends to be described in terms of the structure of the system (such as language), and not in terms of the mental representation of that system. There is increasing evidence that the gap between the domain of a rationalist theory of language and the actual performance of the human actor is increasing. It may therefore be advisable to reject that distinction and to ask for theories that are couched in psychological terms and depend on the characteristic of the human mind for their parameters.

Competence theories are likely to be perfectly valid descriptions of systems *within another domain.* Thus, the structure of language or logic is one domain; whether and how that structure is perceived and incorporated into the human mental apparatus (if it is at all) is an entirely different domain. Psychologists may get some hint of the problems faced by a language or logic user, but the structure of those theories does not define the competence of the human user. The latter may use some or none or all of the structure, but only empirical evidence and creative theory can make that clear (i.e., what is used or not).

The distinction between the structure of a domain and the structure that is mentally represented has been made for the case of story grammars and the mental models of these grammars that people use in representing, telling, and remembering stories.[28] At a simpler level, consider the structure of a house as it is represented in architectural plans. These plans could be used to find one's way around the house, but they are not isomorphic with the structure of that house as it is represented in the mind of one of its inhabitants. The structure of the house *as mentally represented* is what we speak of when we refer to its mental representation.[29] The architectural structure of the house is of interest since it will reveal certain parallels and divergencies from the mental structure, but it is not the underlying competence of the house user. Neither is the structure of a language, *qua* language, a description of the actual or potential competence of its speakers.

---

[28] J.M. Mandler (1984b).

[29] Which, in turn, is different from the underlying representation that generates the mental model.

A similar distinction needs to be applied to our understanding and use of social structures. The structure of a society, of a social group, or of a culture affects the way its member behave and think; it constrains in fact what is doable and thinkable. For example, the structure of a society determines who does what and with what tools; it determines social mobility, and the relations among its races, classes, and other subgroups. On the other hand, there is the structure of that society as it is perceived by its members. Not only is this perception different among different groups and individuals, but it is in part determined by the structure of the society. This perception (or representation) of the structure of a society among its members in turn has effects which can be distinguished from the direct effects of the societal structure *per se.*

ACTION

The idea that even simple behaviors are not just chains of reflexes has occupied psychologists and biologists for some decades. In the following section, I borrow heavily from C. R. Gallistel, who has presented the psychological-biological evidence for the pivotal idea that action sequences are centrally programmed and structured.[30] Building on previous work, Gallistel emphasizes the need to consider higher processes that manage the direction of behavior. The hierarchy of actions and behaviors starts with the "reflexes, endogenous oscillators, taxes, and other functional units of behavior." Nodes at succeeding higher levels control combinations of structures or coordinations represented at the next-lower level. This control is generated by appropriate inhibitory and disinhibitory signals. Organized actions controlled by a particular node have functional significance, that is, they subserve particular functions or goals. However, they do not necessarily, or even usually, involve the serial firing of the identical behavioral constituents. The nodal organization "uses" the appropriate lower constituents so that a particular reflex, for example, may precede another under one organization and follow it under another. At the apex of these hierarchical organizations of actions are nodes that are equivalent to the psychologist's use of the term *motive.* These highest order nodes control the various actions that are usually described as satisfying a particular (usually biological) motive. Stimuli may be received at any level of the hierarchy, but those that activate the apex of a hierarchy are generally equivalent to motivational stimuli. Although Gallistel does not use the term *schema*

---

[30] Gallistel (1974, 1980), and for a voice from the 1950s that prepared the ground for a new view of action, see Lashley (1951).

in this context, the structure of these actions can easily be understood in terms of schema theory.

There are two distinct issues in the organization of actions: the structure of action and the representation of action. The first addresses the structure of action as presented by Gallistel. Leaving aside for the moment the class of preprogrammed, "innate" structures, we note that in the course of its transactions with the environment the organism acquires new complex action structures. These are typically built out of existing units, at the lowest level of reflexes and taxes, but more generally out of any existing organized action units. The conditions under which these new action systems develop are, at least, complex and, to a large extent, unknown in their specifics. For example, (primary) reinforcers may function by inducing or generating the appearance of previously established systems under new "motivational" contexts. A reinforcing event can move an existing action system so that it operates under new conditions. Alternatively, new sensory-motor action structures may develop on the basis of cognitive maps and explorations of new environments.[31] The extensive literature on operant shaping suggests that new action systems may also be generated by "reinforcement" and by the information-seeking explorations of the organism. "Primary" reinforcement is often the occasion for the occurrence of highly organized responses, and the system that is being organized develops out of the extension of these existing "primary" systems.

The continuing exercise (execution) of an action system generates a more tightly organized and invariant structure. For example, a rat learning a maze or humans learning to drive from their office to a new home both eventually develop well-organized action systems that at first are constituted of individual and often previously unrelated subsystems. For example, we may know the way from the freeway to the center of town, and have previously learned how to get from one office to another in town. In the course of developing a way of getting to the new job, these two constituents are then related and integrated. In the course of developing new action structures much hypothesis testing (or so-called trial-and-error behavior) may occur. Potential subsystems may be tested behaviorally or implicitly before a particular combination is found and used. As the new sequence is used consecutively, with less and less variation (error), it establishes its own general structure and organization. But how do we acquire the analogues of subsystems that can be cognitively or behaviorally tried out? This question brings us to the second issue in the organization of action. The distinction here is, for example, between the action system that organizes my use of knives and forks in eating a steak and the fuzzy cognitive representa-

---

[31] Gallistel (1974).

tion I have of those actions. This distinction is, of course, related to the previous discussion of the structure of the world (be it houses or languages) and our representation of it. Only, in the case of action, the distinction is between the organization of action and its execution on the one hand and the actor's perception of that organization on the other.

Once an action is executed, it eventually becomes represented in a second sense in a cognitive structure.[32] In other words, actions, typically efferent motor systems, are represented in two distinct ways: first, in the underlying representation of the action structure itself, the action system just discussed; second, in the representation of our perceptual (primarily visual and kinesthetic) registration of that action. For the sake of brevity, we may call the former *action structures* and the latter *cognitive structures*. Action systems themselves are primarily automatic and not even subject to conscious representation in many cases. Thus, we know how to walk and talk, eat and speak, laugh and cry. The knowledge of the execution of the hierarchies of actions involved in these acts is represented in the action system. We have no direct insight into the sequence of muscle movements and limb and body coordinations that are involved in these complex acts. Nonetheless, we can, in a more general sense, talk about these actions. Our ability to do so depends on schemas that arise out of the execution of the actions themselves. There is, at present, no well-defined explicit way of understanding the relations between the action structures and their secondary schematic representation. Not only can the latter initiate action structures (as in my decision to type this sentence), but they can also be used to interface with and modify existing action systems, as every novice tennis player and coach knows.

Many of our cognitive structures represent this secondary internalization of action. Although much of this representation seems to be in the form of images (tactual and visual), there is no need to restrict the formal character of these structures to one modality or another. The development of the representation of complex response patterns has been demonstrated experimentally.[33] During early stages of training, people could not produce a pattern in the absence of external stimulus support; after moderate training, however, they reported tactual imagery, and after extended overtraining they reported visual imagery of the overt pattern. The development of secondary structures analogous to the structure of the action follows the elimination of errors. After the action systems that generate the structures have stabilized and per-

---

[32] Piaget (1953).

[33] Mandler and Kuhlman (1961).

formance is essentially asymptotic, the representation of the action will be essentially identical from occurrence to occurrence; that is, stable schemas will have developed.

Once such a cognitive structure of action has been developed, it can be used for elaborate choice and decision processes prior to output. What is manipulated is the secondary representation of action and not the action structure directly. Much cognitive activity is involved in the construction of new action systems. During that phase, various separate action units are inspected and tested before they are incorporated into the new action system. Thus, the construction of new systems is characterized by consciousness (e.g., when we consider various alternatives in learning a new skill). Once it has been established, the action runs off without cognitive intervention (i.e., by the activation of the appropriate action system). These new integrated actions will, in turn, become represented as secondary schemas.

What is the relation between existing action systems and the secondary schemas that represent them? It is a generally safe assumption that one of the characteristics of mental life is that a relation is established between any two or more structures that are active at a given time. For example, a relation will exist between old memories of a past meeting that are retrieved when one sees an old friend and the perceptual structure that is operative in constructing the physical conditions of the current meeting with that friend. Given that assumption. a relation will necessarily exist between any action system and its secondary representation, since the action system is by hypothesis active when the secondary representational structure is being established. Furthermore, that relation is likely to be highly stable in that only a specific action system and its cognitive structure have this high correlation between the occurrence of the action system and its secondary "image". Clearly, the two structures are not isomorphic--typically, the cognitive structure will be a degraded, abbreviated version of the action system itself. The relation between the two might be called a pseudoisomorphism. While verbal labels offer only a poor approximation, they do convey the flavor of this abbreviated isomorphism. Consider the relation between "driving home," "making love," "preparing beef Wellington," "writing my name," and the appropriate action systems. It might be noted that these secondary "models" of action frequently incorporate and are shaped by common sense or folk models about what are appropriate and doable actions. What remains obscure is the mechanism whereby the system goes from a cognitive consideration of a possible action system to its execution. Despite the lack of isomorphic structures, a single action system may occur after only some partial activation of its cognitive representation or even in response to just a summary label (e.g., "Draw a dog" or "Tie your shoelaces"). To say that such a sequence involves the relation between an action structure and a (secondary) cognitive structure is only to restate the hoary problem about the relation between thought and action. It still needs to be spelled out how changes in one of them affect changes in the other. Clearly, we do learn about changing our action systems via the cognitive structures, for example, when we are instructed to execute a tennis serve as if we were swatting a fly or a gymnastic exercise by imagining that our feet are cemented to the floor.

The relation between action structures and their secondary representation in cognitive ones finds its parallel in the mental models that we construct about our environment, its technology, artifacts, and science.[34] These mental models have a function similar to the mental models we construct about ourselves; their "major purpose. . .is to enable [us] to predict the operation of the target system."[35] As our cognitive schemas are adjusted and changed, we become better able to understand how our body works and why and how we do the things we do. It is also the secondary representations of actions that make possible evaluations of our own actions. When judging or evaluating others, we often derive evaluative judgments from our observations of their actions. When we, maybe too infrequently, evaluate our own actions we are again often dependent on our perceptions of those actions, i.e.,our self-perceptions. But these perceptions are themselves constructed out of the secondary schemas of those acts. Depending on how such secondary perceptual schemas have been constructed, we can perceive ourselves as being aggressive or helpful, cooperative or competitive, and so forth. Our schema *about* an action will determine how we evaluate it. These secondary self-perceptions are in turn important building blocks in the construction of our notions of the self and the emotional experiences that derive from the evaluative states.

The distinction between action schemas and their secondary representation maps directly into the distinction between procedural and declarative knowledge alluded to earlier. Actions are, by definition, procedures, and procedural knowledge, just like an action system, is frequently not accessible to conscious knowledge, for it cannot, in contrast to declarative knowledge, be spoken. Secondary schemas, as discussed here, have the advantage of providing declarative access to procedural knowledge. I can speak and think about the fact that I know how to tie my shoelaces, double-clutch my car, or prepare an omelet without having access to the detailed procedures involved.

---

[34] Gentner and Stevens (1982), see also Johnson-Laird (1983).

[35] Norman (1982).

DIVERGENCIES, DIRECTIONS, AND DIALECTICS

The rapid development of a "cognitive" view of human beings has spawned a variety of directions and divergencies. Many of these, in a Hegelian spiral, repeat themes of previous psychologies. Of particular interest are those that insist on context (stimulus) specificity and those that appeal to a nativist/formalist view of human nature.

The contextualist position has a number of versions, and I can hardly do justice to all of them here. The general point is that human thought and action is usually context specific, determined by the requirements and demands of the immediate environment and context. Formally, that position is best illustrated by the theories of James Gibson and the neo-Gibsonians, with their insistence on direct perception and the unmediated determination of phenomenal experience by physical variables.[36] In the field of memory, the contextualist argument has been exemplified by Tulving's early statements of the encoding specificity principle, i.e., that recovery of a memorial content depends on the presence of the cues that were specifically present at the time of encoding.[37]

On the other hand, the 1970s saw the emergence of sociobiology and also the formalist/rationalist view of the human mind. Both tend to depict an essentially powerless human being, subject to the forces of an unalterable (at least within a human time frame) biology and destiny. Sociobiology prescribes how we can act; formalism, how we can think. The ideology is one of human passivity and powerlessness--the world is as it is, and we can only find out what it is that we are permitted by laws of biology and rationality to think and do.

One of the more extreme statements in the, rather old, rationalist/formalist tradition comes from Fodor's revival of faculty psychology, though his selective use of evidence suggests that it is more a faculty philosophy.[38] In insisting on a system that is both an encapsulated set of faculties *and* innate, Fodor pictures a rigid organism, strongly dependent on the limits of the world that it may analyze and the specific abilities with which it is endowed. Fodor's modular input systems are elusive machines whose characteristics change from page to page, assisted by central processors and transistors that seem to have

---

[36] For example, Gibson (1966), Turvey (1977).

[37] Tulving (1983), see also Norman and Bobrow (1979). See also Chapter 4.

[38] It is interesting to note that Fodor's language of the mind was, in 1983, more closely tied to the computer metaphor than that of any contemporary psychological theorist.

unlimited freedom to cope with embarrassing examples counter to the modular position. His conclusion, though, is unequivocal: "[N]o facts . . . contradict the claim that the neural mechanisms subserving input analysis develop according to specific, endogenously determined patterns under the impact of environmental releasers." and "[T]hese mechanisms are instantiated in correspondingly specific, hardwired neural structures." and "[M]uch of the information at the disposal of such systems is innately specified . . . ."[39]

There is a trivial sense in which analyzers are in fact modular, i.e., systems that are input specific and highly specialized. The sensory systems themselves and the analytic mechanisms that process their output are of course specific to the sensory modality. For example, the visual system processes information in parallel, but the auditory system does not; visual, auditory, and kinesthetic information comes in different packages as it occurs in the world and creates different kinds of representations (see the earlier section on "World and Mind"). However, once information is obtained by the analyzers, it becomes available to the mental systems as a whole and is often subject to mechanisms that are shared and also interchangeable among modalities. For example, consider instances of synesthesia, or the ability of human beings to match intensities across modalities, or the combinatorial function of constructive consciousness discussed in Chapter 3. Specific input analyzers are made up of innate mechanisms and experiential strategies, sometimes restricted to modalities, at other times available across modalities. On the other hand, humans are frequently able to develop new skills and automatic analyses that act, in their finished form, very much like Fodor's modules. The alternatives are NOT a modular system that strictly defines faculties and abilities on the one hand and a generalized analyzer and inductive mechanism on the other. All the evidence is that the very plasticity of the human mind speaks to a mixed economy of mechanisms and processes.[40] Even neurophysiological evidence suggests both plasticity and, for example, multiple (and different) representations of the sensory world.[41]

---

[39] Fodor (1983, pp.100-101).

[40] Much of the modular argument speaks for the notion of "direct perception" of James Gibson and his descendants.

[41] Merzenich et al. (1984), Woolsey (1981-82).

I do not wish to write at length about the Gibsonian movement, except to characterize it as one of the directions that has adopted rather rigid notions of stimulus-response mappings. Gibson and his collaborators have provided us with exciting and important evidence about the characteristics of the external world that direct and determine human perception. They have been less successful in the area of memory and problem solving, for example, but their emphasis on perception has made it possible for them to speak about direct correspondences between perception and the physical world. In contrast to "cognitive" positions that see perception as constructed and "indirect," the ecological view of Gibson insists on "direct," unmediated connections between physical events in the world and phenomenal experiences. The insistence that the information available in the external world specifies perception can be contrasted with early cognitive views of cognitive structures as determining what can be perceived--to the extent of claiming that an event that is completely discrepant with current active schemas or structures is imperceivable. Neither extreme position appears to be tenable, but their contributions should not be slighted. James Gibson and his descendants remind us that we do live in a real, physical world, whose texture and gradients and patterns are reflected in our view of that world.

Some recent demonstrations in perception help us find more appropriate solutions to these extreme views. James Cutting has used the notion of "directed perception." He argues that we live in a world rich in information that is potentially available for perceptual pickup or analyses, but that the organism selects only parts of that rich array. For example, different physical gradients (such as perspective, compression, and density) are used in the analysis of flat as distinct from curved surfaces.[42]

The human mental apparatus undoubtedly is endowed with a number of innate analytic systems, as well as similarly innate modes of acting. These represent the most primitive and the minimum necessary in order to engage in a transaction with the external world. These systems develop and become active as such transactions occur and specific analyzers and actions come to be arranged in special ways for dealing with special problems (and thus gain the appearance of Fodorian modules). It is patently obvious that human language is peculiar to humans, presumably determined in part by bits and pieces of biology accumulated over the ages into the apparent unity of "language." But there is no direct evidence for a single language faculty independent of the various mental mechanisms (biological and experiential) that it shares with other functions. The evolutionary history of our primitive

---

[42] Cutting and Millard (1984) and Cutting (in preparation).

mental mechanisms is presumably one that has maximized their ability to interact with the world and to produce a functioning organism that is both effective and highly adaptable and pliable. The mature mental apparatus is the result of a dialectic between given and emerging mechanisms on the one hand and the evidence and demand of the external world on the other.[43]

No biological or environmental constraints fully determine human thought and action, but neither does any schema or cognitive structure. To say that a particular set of actions is contextually constrained is to say that we are able to develop mental structures that respond, when necessary, to the specific demands and conditions of certain contexts and environments. To say that perceptual schemas determine what is seeable is to say that we have developed structures that constrain our analyses of certain physical events. Our evolutionary history has apparently provided us with certain physical and behavioral structures that have made us more adaptive; it has also provided us fortuitously with structures whose "adaptive" uses do not arise out of their evolutionary history directly (such as hands for writing and legs for kicking goals). Most important, the (very slow) process of evolution has created an organism that often has available many ways of achieving the same function, that is highly "adaptive" in that sense, that has "fail safe" ways of coping with the demands of a real world, and that continuously benefits from cultural evolution and adaptation in finding new ways of coping.

Finally, we need to explore the varied use of the concept of *goals* in cognitive science. As I noted in Chapter 1, the artificial intelligence community in particular has insisted on cognitive structures that are driven by the goals set by those structures. I do not argue that such goals and goalsettings are either useless or imaginary; on the contrary, I believe that the analysis of goals has been slighted in the past and deserves more detailed attention. However, there is a variety of different situations and tasks in which "goals" are invoked, and these contexts require quite different analyses. *First*, there are thought and action sequences with *inevitable outcomes* that seem to act as goals. Consider such mundane activities as brushing one's teeth, cooking an omelet, dialing a familiar telephone number. These activities are usually automatic, and they run off in a ballistic fashion. They are frequently not set off by the "goal" they achieve (clean teeth, a finished omelet, reaching a friend), but usually are initiated by internal or external conditions that are part of a larger plan. Once the initiating conditions exist, the activity runs off automatically, often as part of a more general plan or schema. *Second*, there are goals that are set by our *physical*

---

[43] I shall return to Piaget's invention of assimilation and accommodation as mechanisms for the realization of that dialectic relationship in Chapter 4.

needs and phenomenal desires. For example, when one is hungry a variety of different possible action schemas is activated, all of which may "satisfy" the goal of terminating one's hunger.[44] Even within that category there are some variations. One may, for example, have a desire for raspberry filled chocolate bonbons. Here the desire or goal is satisfied by a very specific object, and alternate routes may not be acceptable. *Finally*, there are so-called set goals in which some thought or action sequence is satisfied only when a particular *outcome is achieved.* Activation of the relevant and often alternative schemas is maintained until such time as the set goal is achieved. Examples are catching a long fly ball, finding a reference, and, in the nonhuman world, the behavior of a heat seeking missile.[45] In short, to invoke a goal as an explanatory device for some human thought or action is not enough; we need to specify how the goal in that situation is operating and how it affects thought and action.

---

[44] See Gallistel (1980) for a discussion of motives as high level plans.

[45] See Bowlby (1969) for a discussion of set goals as well as the problem of goal setting in general.

CHAPTER 3

Consciousness

The study of consciousness has started to regain its rightful place in the psychological enterprise. There may not be general agreement with the proposition that consciousness is the central problem of a human cognitive psychology; however, enough people have started to worry about the problem, and many others feel obliged at least to consider it.[1]

Two attitudes toward consciousness bound the extremes of the discussion to follow. One considers consciousness to be ineffable and unapproachable as a scientific enterprise; the other sees it within the grasp of current technology. The former, behaviorist formulation made its escape from knotty problems by asserting that consciousness is epiphenomenal, an uninteresting and functionally impotent byproduct of

---

[1] This chapter is a descendant of my chapter on "Consciousness: Respectable, useful, and probably necessary" (1975a), revised as Chapter 3 of "Mind and emotion" (1975c). An extension and summary was presented in "The construction and limitation of consciousness" (1984c), and another recapitulation was written as Chapter 4 of "Mind and body" (1984b). A previous version of this chapter was presented in Mandler (1983).

observable behaviors.[2] The other view, sometimes derived from current artificial intelligence endeavors and the theory of automata, asserts its domain over consciousness by suggesting possible relations between consciousness and computing machines.

Arguments against the behaviorist position cannot be based merely on the rejection of the epiphenomenal arguments or on the assertion that modern approaches make the study of consciousness possible. Rather, it should be shown, as it surely can, that consciousness does in fact have important functions in human thought and action. The behaviorist critique of consciousness was more an avoidance than a critique, a point made also by Skinner,[3] who bravely tackled the problem of these "private events." We should pay attention to his argument because it does not deny conscious events. Rather Skinner finds them mostly unnecessary "waystations" between stimuli and behavior. And his assertion that some of our intentions and thoughts, rather than being initiators of actions, are often glosses on ongoing or incipient actions needs to be taken seriously. What we need to show is not just that the behaviorists' analyses fail to do justice to human consciousness, but to demonstrate positively what it is that consciousness DOES, what it is needed for, what we cannot and would not do or think if there were no such mechanism.

There is a subset of the arguments about the inefficacy of consciousness that is related to the mind-body question of how mind might cause bodily states. At least some of the various philosophical "solutions" to the mind-body problem make conscious contents ineffective in a causal chain. A psychological argument about conscious inefficacy has been made on the basis that "awareness often occurs *after* the events or the actions that Mind might be supposed to control."[4] I shall argue later that an important effect of consciousness is actually to be found in events *subsequent* to the occurrence of the aware state.

The issue of possible conscious states of computers requires a different argument. Consider a comparison between two questions: first, whether computers can be conscious, and, second, whether they can be pregnant. The latter question is ridiculous because we know that in order to be pregnant one needs certain equipment and that certain prior conditions must be fulfilled. Computers neither have the equipment nor can they engage in the prior activities necessary for pregnancy. In the case of consciousness, we have little knowledge

---

[2] The assignment of consciousness to an epiphenomenal byproduct of human mental life is not restricted to behaviorists, see for example Harnad (1982).

[3] See for example Skinner (1964).

[4] Gregory (1981, p. 474, emphasis added).

about the equipment or conditions necessary in order to reach that state. It is this absence of knowledge, this ignorance, that makes the question reasonable for some. However, if one first were to consider what it is that "being conscious" implies in terms of processes and equipment, one might be able to ask the question sensibly. At the present time, it is an empty question.

The more generalized form of the computer claim is that consciousness may be a property of certain classes of automata. Philip Johnson-Laird has suggested that "human consciousness depends on intentionality and self-awareness; and they in turn depend on . . . a recursive embedding of a model of the self within the self so that the different embeddings are accessible *in parallel* to the operating system." Johnson-Laird argues for mind as a parallel automaton that contains a model of itself, with conscious contents being the values of parameters that serve as input and output to the operating system. Consciousness "is a property of a certain class of parallel algorithms." This computational view of consciousness makes available high level models of our world; it makes possible "conscious decisions about those matters that govern our behaviour."[5] It is, however, not quite clear why *conscious* decisions about these important matters are functionally superior to unconscious ones. Would that sentence be any less persuasive if the word "conscious" were left out? The arguments are compelling that it is very *convenient* to have such things as conscious states, but I argue that they have other important functions that contribute to the decision process itself.

The proper question is NOT whether computers can be conscious or whether certain automata might display conscious-like characteristics, but what theoretical account we can give for consciousness. Given such a satisfactory account, we may ask whether we can simulate consciousness on a computer. If one were to assert that computers can be conscious, one would have to specify how that function is achieved or to imply that the equipment (as in pregnancy) is comparable to human constituents. The question about computer consciousness is sometimes asked because some of our software generates products that look like conscious products. But a question about simulating consciousness asks in the first instance what it is that we want to simulate.

---

5 Johnson-Laird (1983, pp.474-476).

The renewed interest in consciousness has been informed in important ways by careful analyses of its occurrences and explorations of its implications.[6] In addition, attempts to understand its role have played a part in practically all the various strands that have produced modern cognitive psychology. Generally, consciousness has been assigned an essentially passive role in the information flow. Thus, George Miller asserted that it is "the *result* of thinking . . . that appears spontaneously in consciousness."[7] Neisser saw focal attention (or consciousness) as facilitating, but not directly influencing, decision processes and the interrogation of the products of different systems.[8]

A more active view than Neisser's was implied by early information processing models that viewed consciousness as a central controlling system.[9] Similar and more explicit suggestions have been made recently in the context of a central "information exchange", which services (unconscious) distributed special processors and produces a "stable and coherent global representation that provides information to the nervous system as a whole . . . ."[10]

Current positions generally subscribe to an active view of conscious states and processes.[11] One of the early versions of these views is the theoretical account of automatic activation and conscious processing contributed by Posner and his associates.[12] The conscious processing discussed by Posner and Snyder is "a mechanism of limited capacity which may be directed toward different types of activity."[13] Consciousness is "directed toward" an unconscious structure or process which then becomes "conscious."

---

6 For example, Natsoulas (1970, 1977).

7 Miller (1962), see also Lashley (1923).

8 Neisser (1967).

9 For example, Atkinson and Shiffrin (1968).

10 Baars (1983).

11 For example, Marcel (1983b), Norman and Shallice (1980), Shallice (1972).

12 For example, Posner and Boies (1971), Posner and Snyder (1975).

13 Posner and Snyder (1975, p.64).

These various positions on consciousness can be divided into those that follow the traditional view that conscious contents occur when a structure is pushed, pulled, or illuminated into consciousness,[14] and those that state that only the results or consequences of mental processes are conscious.[15] What all of them have in common is some implication of identity or overlap between consciousness and (focal) attention.

THE PROBLEM OF PRIVATE EXPERIENCES

The individual experiences feelings, attitudes, thoughts, images, ideas, beliefs, and other contents of consciousness, but these contents are not accessible to anyone else. Briefly stated, it is not possible to build a phenomenal psychology that is shared. A *theory* of phenomena may be shared, but once private consciousness is expressed in words, gestures, or in any way externalized, it becomes necessarily a transformation of the private experience. No theory external to the individual (i.e., one that treats the organism as the object of observation, description, and explanation) can, at the same time, be a theory that uses private experiences, feelings, and attitudes as data.[16] Events and objects in consciousness can never be available to the observer without having been restructured, reinterpreted, and appropriately modified. The content of consciousness, as philosophers and psychologists have told us for centuries, is not directly available as a datum in psychology.

Can the perennial problem of private datum and public inference at least be stated concisely in order to indicate the magnitude of the problem?

There are two related problems in the study of consciousness. First, not only may the nature of the interrogation affect the reported content of consciousness but, more basically, the act of examination itself may affect the individually observable conscious contents, since the conscious act of interrogating one's conscious content must occupy some part of the limited capacity. As a result, the available content is altered by the process of interrogation. We are faced with a phenomenon that might be called the uncertainty principle of psychology: "The particular difficulty that the questioner may influence

---

[14] For example, Freud (1900), Posner and Snyder (1975), Shallice (1972).

[15] For example, Lashley (1923), Miller (1962), Mandler (1975a).

[16] Gray (1971).

the answer recalls the uncertainty principle in physics, which limits the knowledge we can gain about any individual particle".[17]

The second problem to be faced is the fact that the contents of consciousness are not simply reproducible by some one-to-one mapping onto verbal report. Even if these contents were always couched in language (which they are not), some theory of transmission would be required. As a result, we are faced, on the one hand, with the individual's awareness of the conscious state and, on the other, with the psychologist's theoretical inference about those contents, on the basis of whatever data, including introspective reports, are available. Both sorts of knowledge may be used as relevant to the construction of a psychology of cognition, although it may in principle be impossible to determine, in any exact sense, the relation between these two interpretations of consciousness.

Private experiences are important aspects of the fully functioning mental system. It is possible to get transformed reports about those events, and it should be possible to develop appropriate theories that relate the contents of consciousness, their transformations, and their report. However, it is not possible to build a *viable* theory that makes precise predictions about private experience, since the outcome of those predictions cannot be properly evaluated by the psychologist-observer.

This position does admit the development of private theories, by individuals, about themselves. To the individual, one's experience *is* a datum, and consequently personal theories about one's own structures are, within limits, testable by direct experience. These individual, personal theories of the self are both pervasive and significant in explaining human action, but they cannot, without peril, be generalized to others or to the species as a whole.[18]

The fact that people develop representations not only *of* their perceptions, thoughts, and actions but also *about* these products is by now well established. I have discussed these secondary schemas in Chapter 2; they are pervasive, and what is available to consciousness is frequently such a secondary schema about our thoughts and actions, represented in personal theories and beliefs. What is represented in consciousness often is not a reflection of the operating processes and structures at all.

---

17 Adrian (1966).

18 Mandler and Mandler (1974).

THE CONSTRUCTION OF CONSCIOUS EXPERIENCE

A new approach to the occurrence of consciousness, developed by A.J. Marcel[19] in the context of perceptual phenomena, has great promise for the development of a new model of consciousness. I have tried to indicate some of the steps, starting with Marcel's initial insights. Marcel is concerned with structures and the conditions under which they reach the conscious state. However, in contrast to the view that structures *become* conscious so that consciousness is simply a different state of a structure, Marcel sees consciousness as a constructive process in which the phenomenal experience is a specific construction to which previously activated schemas have contributed.[20] Marcel relates his position to the rejection of the identity assumption, which postulates that conscious states are to be seen as merely another state of a preconscious structure. The identity position characterizes practically all current views of consciousness, which postulate that some preconscious state "breaks through," "reaches," "is admitted," "crosses a threshhold," "enters," into consciousness. A constructivist position states, in contrast, that most conscious states are constructed out of those preconscious structures in response to the requirements of the moment.

We can be conscious only of experiences that are constructed out of activated schemas. We are not conscious of the process of activation or the constituents of the activated schemas. A constructed conscious experience depends on the activated schemas of one or more of the constituent processes and features. The schemas that are available to constructive consciousness must be adequately activated and must not be inhibited. The resulting phenomenal experience is "an attempt to make sense of as much data as possible at the highest or most functionally useful level possible . . . ."[21]

---

[19] Marcel (1983b).

[20] See also Treisman and Gelade (1980) for a constructive view of focal attention which is very similar to Marcel's proposition.

[21] Marcel (1983b). A similar interpretation of consciousness was advanced by E. Roy John (in Thatcher and John (1977, pp. 294-304). He noted that in consciousness "information about multiple individual modalities of sensation and perception is combined into a unified multidimensional representation," i.e., that "consciousness itself is a representational system."

If I become aware of a dog, I may not be conscious of his teeth unless a relevant growl shifts the current conscious construction. The teeth may well have activated the relevant schemas, but these do not enter automatically into consciousness. We are customarily conscious of the important aspects of the environs, but never conscious of all the evidence that enters the sensory gateways or of all our potential knowledge of the event.[22] A number of experiments have shown that people may be aware of what are usually considered higher order aspects of an event without being aware of its constituents. Thus, subjects are sometimes able to specify the category membership of a word without being aware of the specific meaning or even the occurrence of the word itself.[23] A similar disjunction between the awareness of categorical and event-specific information has been reported for some clinical observations.[24]

This approach to consciousness suggests highly selective constructions that may be either abstract/general or concrete/specific, depending on what is appropriate to current needs and demands. It is also consistent with arguments that claim immediate access to complex meanings of events. These higher order "meanings" will be readily available whenever the set is to find a relatively abstract construction, a situation frequent in our daily interactions with the world.[25] In general, it seems to be the case that "we are aware of [the] significance [of a set of cues] instead of and before we are aware of the cues."[26]

Conscious constructions represent the most general interpretation that is appropriate to the current scene in keeping with both the intentions of the individual and the demands of the environment. In the absence of any specific requirements (internally or externally generated), the current construction will be the most general (or abstract) available. Thus, we are aware of looking at a landscape when viewing the land from a mountaintop, but we become aware of a particular road when asked how we might get down or of an approaching storm when some dark clouds "demand" inclusion in the current construction. In a problem-solving task, we are conscious of those current mental products that are closest to the task at hand, i.e., the likely solution to the problem.

---

[22] See also Köhler (1929).

[23] Marcel (1983a), Fowler, Wolford, Slade, and Tassinary (1981).

[24] For example, Warrington (1975).

[25] Lazarus (1981).

[26] Marcel (1983b).

WHEN ARE WE CONSCIOUS AND WHAT ARE WE CONSCIOUS OF?

What are the most obvious occasions for conscious constructions? First, we are often conscious in the process of acquiring new knowledge and behavior. While not all new learning is conscious, the construction of complex action sequences and the acquisition or restructuring of knowledge require conscious participation. In the adult, thoughts and actions typically are conscious before they become well integrated and subsequently automatic. Learning to drive a car is a conscious process, whereas the skilled driver acts automatically and unconsciously. It follows that conscious evaluations of one's actions should more often reflect those mental and behavioral events that are in the process of being acquired or learned and less often the execution of automatic sequences.[27] In fact, there is some evidence that subjective estimates of mental workload are correlated with indices of performance on unpracticed novel tasks but unrelated to the performance of well-practiced, familiar ones.[28]

The sequence from conscious to unconscious is not ubiquitous. It is reversed in the infant[29] and apparently is reversed in simple adult functions, such as in perceptual learning and in the acquisition of some simple motor skills, where skills learned unconsciously may only subsequently be represented in consciousness. The products of such acquisitions also may be divided into conscious and unconscious ones, a distinction that is found in the division between declarative and procedural knowledge. In addition, shifts from unconscious to conscious processing occur frequently. For example, the pianist will acquire skills in playing chords and trills and in reading music that are at first consciously represented but then become unconscious. However, the analytic (conscious) mode is used when the accomplished artist practices a particular piece for a concert, when conscious access becomes necessary to achieve the proper emphases, phrasings, and tempi. One wonders to what extent this process is similar to that seen in the psychoanalytic encounter, where automatic (unadaptive?) ways of dealing with the world are the object of a conscious theory of their

---

[27] For an early and a late statement of this conclusion, see Bain (1875, p. 541) and J.R. Anderson (1982).

[28] D. Gopher, personal communication.

[29] J.M. Mandler (1984a).

function and then become accessible for conscious repair and change.

Second, conscious processes are frequently active during the exercise of choices and judgments, particularly with respect to action requirements. These choices, often novel ones, require the consideration of possible outcomes and consequences and frequently involve what the behaviorist literature calls "covert trial and error." However, it seems unreasonable to postulate that a conscious state exists only when selections are required. How do we account for our continuous consciousness of the surround? I suggest, as a first approximation, that a state of consciousness exists that is constructed out of the most general structures currently being activated by current concerns and environmental requirements. It provides, in consciousness, a specification in abstract terms of where we are and what we are doing there. Choice and selectivity will then produce changes in that current "reflection" of the state of the world.

Third, conscious processes exercise an important function during "troubleshooting." Thus, relevant aspects of the world are brought into consciousness when automatic structures somehow fail in their functions, when a particular habitual way of acting fails, or when a thought process cannot be brought to an appropriate conclusion. Experienced drivers become "aware" of where they are and what they are doing when something new and different happens; when a near miss, a police car, or an unexpected traffic light is suddenly registered. The troubleshooting function of consciousness permits repair of current troublesome or injudicious processing and subsequent choice from among other alternatives. These arguments stress the role of consciousness in action, in contrast to a contemplative, reflective view of conscious states. A similar approach has been suggested for the role of consciousness in the execution and voluntary initiation of actions[30] and in its association with "predictive inadequacy or failure."[31]

These various suggestions, already distilled from a longer list I presented a decade ago, can be brought under a general rule for changes in conscious states. *When current conscious constructions do not account for the state of the world, then a new conscious state will be initiated.*[32] The adequacy of current constructions is usually indexed by discrepancies and competition among alternatives arising either out of external activations (and demands) or out of intrapsychic interchanges. A current conscious state will be changed if it does not account for (make sense of) a situation in which the available alternatives fail to

---

[30] Norman and Shallice (1980).

[31] Gregory (1981).

[32] Assuming of course that attention is allocated to the world at all.

meet some criterion for action or problem solving. Such a state will, of course, also change whenever an external event indexes the inadequacy of current thought or action. Our expectations may be violated when the environment keeps changing or when some external piece of evidence cannot be assimilated. Change is defined in terms of our current conscious state and the particular events that are acceptable (expected) within that state. A jogger who may not notice (be conscious of) others along the path because they have always been encountered before will become aware of an elephant. On the other hand the jogger who revels in the loneliness of the long distance runner may well become aware of intrusive others, whether elephants or not. When the environment is constant, we respond to internal demands and use those for conscious constructions. Daydreamers are unaware of their surrounds, until a shout or a raindrop demand to be accounted for in the stream of consciousness.

In other words, the contents of consciousness change whenever there is a change in the state of the world, defined as any change in the sensory evidence or in intentions, instructions, context, or situation. Spatiotemporal attentional adjustments take place whenever there is movement in the environment, when there is a change in the current state of the world. These changes can be indexed by changes in the conscious state or by (unconscious) adjustments to the locus of changes (e.g., in eye movements). I discuss later the latter mechanisms under the rubric of attention. However, I should say here that the first kind of mechanism, the general state-of-the-world consciousness, may also be constructed in response to the demands and variables that govern strictly attentional events. The world is always in a state of flux, and change in the environment may demand new conscious constructions. The results of such activity will be the most abstract, general kind of representation consonant with the intentions and requirements of the moment, unless some specific change is so intense and relevant to current functioning that it requires more concrete, special focusing and new conscious constructions. From that point of view, the continuous state of consciousness is simply a reflection of a dynamic, changing environment. As I sit in a restaurant, enjoying good food and good company, I am conscious of food or conversation at a level that reflects my current interest and intentions, until somebody spills soup over my back and consciousness radically focuses to that event.

It appears that one of the functions of the conscious construction is to bring two or more (previously unconscious) mental contents into direct juxtaposition. The phenomenal experience of choice seems to demand exactly such an occurrence. We usually do not refer to a choice unless there is a "conscious" choice between two or more alternatives. The attribute of "choosing" is applied to a decision process regarding two items on a menu, several television programs, or two or

more careers, but not to the process that decides whether to start walking across a street with the right or the left foot, whether to scratch
one's ear with a finger or with the ball of the hand, or whether to take
one or two sips from a cup of hot coffee. The former cases involve the
necessity of deciding between two or more alternatives, whereas the
latter involve only the situationally predominant action. However,
given a cup of hot coffee, I may "choose" to take one very small sip, or
I may "choose" to start with my right foot in a 100-meter race, given
certain information that it will improve my time for the distance. In
other words, for some alternatives that are usually selected unconsciously, special conditions, such as possible consequences and social factors, may make it possible for conscious constructions to be involved and to make those choices "conscious" too.

Choosing is carried out by complex unconscious mechanisms that
have direct connections with and relations to action systems and other
executive systems. Consciousness permits the redistribution of activations, so that the choice mechanism operates on the basis of new values
of schemas and structures that have been produced (activated) in the
conscious state. The mechanisms that select certain actions among
alternatives are not themselves conscious, but the conditions for new
choices are created consciously, thus giving the appearance of conscious
free choices and operations of the will.[33] What consciousness does
permit is the running through of potential actions and choices, the
coexistence of alternative outcomes, the changing of weightings of
currently active schemas in the direction of one that promises greater
likelihood of success, and so forth. The simultaneous presence in a
conscious state of several different mental contents makes possible the
establishment of new associations, and the emergence of previously
quiescent cognitive structures, now activated by the conscious structures. In problem-solving activities, our consciousness of various alternatives, of trying out solutions, is often taken for the process that
determines the final outcome. Although these conscious activities are
no doubt related to the unconscious activations and processing that they
influence, they are at best not the only forces that directly determine
actions. Their similarity, in many situations, to those unconscious ones
leads one to conclude that thought determines actions directly, but
thought, defined as conscious mental contents, is in one sense truly
epiphenomenal and in another determinative of action. It determines
further unconscious processes but is several steps removed from the actual processes that pervade our mental life. Conscious thoughts are approximations of those unconscious events, in fact the best available,
but they are no substitute for the representations and processes that

---

33 See Norman and Shallice (1980).

need to be postulated for an eventual understanding of human action and thought.

The account I give here is intended primarily to account for changes in the contents of consciousness; it does not address itself to the other sense of consciousness, i.e., the distinction between being conscious or not as a continuing state. The state of "being conscious" (as distinct from being unconscious and unreceptive to any internal or external evidence) implies some continuously activated mental structures that define the current state of our world and the expectations that such structures always generate.

Having listed some of the conditions that give rise to conscious states, we can appreciate better the relation of these conditions to the constructivist approach. In general there are three characteristics of the human mind that are active in the construction of conscious contents and that contribute to efficient and constructive thought and problem solving. These characteristics are schema activation, the constructive nature of mental events, and the limitation of conscious experience.

CONSCIOUSNESS AND INTROSPECTION

The constructive approach to consciousness is also relevant to speculations about the nature of introspective (verbal) reports. Ericsson and Simon[34] have provided an excellent theoretical account of the generation of such reports. However, their account is concerned primarily with the relationship between information available in short term memory (STM) on the one hand and verbalized information on the other. STM seems to operate as a (more respectable?) substitute for consciousness. "Attended to," "heeded," and "stored in STM" are used as synonymous expressions; recently attended information is assumed to be kept in STM and is "directly accessible" for producing verbal reports; but the products of automatic processing are not available to STM. The question of what it is that is available in STM (-consciousness) is never specifically addressed, but it is implied that that information somehow directly represents cognitive processes. In contrast, I argue that these "available" contents of STM are themselves the product of constructive processes. A theory of introspection needs to specify how "heeding" and "attending" operate and also how such processes determine (construct) specific conscious contents.

---

[34] Ericsson and Simon (1980).

Whenever a conscious content is constructed that seeks to recover an intrapsychic series of events that occurred some time in the past, it should be obvious that such constructions will be influenced by current as well as past activations. As a result, introspective reports will very often reflect not what "actually" happened, but rather what is the most reasonable construction at the moment of introspection.[35]

What determines what it is that is constructed? After all, what makes sense in one situation may not in another. Furthermore, what is functionally useful may be very specific, such as knowing where the butter is usually kept in the refrigerator, or quite general, such as knowing that butter knives are not appropriate for slicing cucumber. The major sources of calling for a particular construction are current tasks and contexts, intentions, and needs. Just as current perceptions are, within schema theory, seen as the result of both external evidence and internal processes (top down and bottom up), so is consciousness in general determined by activated higher order structures as well as by the evidence of the surrounds. Interactive, reverberative top down and bottom up processes are usually conceptualized as the instantiation of schemas that receive initial activation from external evidence and, once activated, become selective in the direction and inhibition of activation. In contrast, structures that represent intentions and interpretations of situational requirements are activated primarily "top down"; they depend on prior evaluations and activations of situational identifications and interpretations of current needs and goals. They need not receive activation from the physical evidence of our surrounds. These structures depend primarily on interpreted evidence, on information about requirements and needs. In the normal course of events it is such more abstract and general structures that define what we are doing, what we want to do, and need to do. Their special role is to satisfy situational and intentional demands. As I have noted earlier, it is only when task and intention are narrowed down to particulars that less general and more specific schemas determine conscious constructions.

We must make a distinction between an intention as a theoretical and as a subjective state of affairs. As a theoretical state, it embodies the idea of a goal, a future state of the world. However, subjective *awareness* of intentions may or may not parallel that theoretical state. Subjective intentions may frequently be mere personal, often verbal, glosses on an ongoing sequence of action. People, as well as chickens, may cross the road in order to get to the other side, but they may just as frequently undertake the crossing because it is activated by some event on the other side, such as chickenfeed or a lighted store window.

---

[35] Nisbett and Wilson (1977).

Consciousness is selective and responsive to both conscious and unconscious intentions. Its contents are obviously highly variable from time to time. One of the reasons for the rapid temporal change is that *only one conscious construction can be experienced at any one point in time.* The well-known ambiguous figures (whether ascending and descending staircases or young and old women) present one case where only one conscious construction for a given physical configuration is experienced, even though we know that two different ones are possible. A similar phenomenon occurs in the case of polysemous words. We know that the word "table" can refer to an object that occurs in rooms or one that occurs in books, but we cannot think of the two meanings simultaneously. On the other hand, when two separate objects are involved (as in the case of "A table of figures is on the dining room table") we have no difficulty in constructing a *single* conscious content. The difference does not seem to be that one interpretation is not possible under the current context,[36] but rather that two interpretations of *the same event* cannot be constructed in consciousness at the same time.

We are apparently never conscious of all the available evidence that surrounds us, but only of a small subset. What is the nature of that limitation?

THE LIMITATION OF CONSCIOUS EXPERIENCE

How much of our current surround or internal events can we represent in consciousness? Momentary consciousness clearly is limited, and one adaptive consequence of that limitation is explored in the next section. At the heart of historical concerns with conscious limitation is the realization that only a few (no more than about six) "objects" can be apprehended by the mind at any one time.[37] William James firmly established the limited capacity concept as a cornerstone of our knowledge about consciousness/attention and G.A. Miller[38] made it a central thesis of modern approaches to human information processing.

---

[36] Baars (1983).

[37] In modern times this was established by the French philosophers Charles Bonnet (1720-1793) and Antoine Louis Claude Destutt de Tracy (1754-1836); and William Hamilton (1859) noted that it applied to both single objects and groupings of objects.

[38] Miller (1956).

The limited capacity of attention should be an excellent candidate for an innate characteristic of human beings. Our colleagues who are often overly eager to ascribe evolutionary and genetic origins to a variety of human characteristics and differences might well focus on limited conscious capacity, which is found across groups, societies, races, and even ages. "[T]here is little or no evidence of either individual or developmental differences in [attentional] capacity . . ." defined as the limited amount of attention that is available "for activating internal units stored in long-term memory."[39]

Such a general characteristic of human functioning as limited attentional capacity should have an important role to play in thought and action. I assume in the first place that the limited capacity characteristic of consciousness serves to reduce further the "blooming confusion" that the physical world potentially presents to the organism. Just as sensory end organs and central transducers radically reduce and categorize the world of physical stimuli to the functional stimuli that are in fact registered, so does the conscious process further reduce the available information to a small and manageable subset. I assume, somewhat circularly, that the limitation of conscious capacity defines what is in fact cognitively manageable. Although we do not know why the reduction is of the magnitude that we observe, it is reasonable to assume that some reduction is necessary. Just consider a process of serial pairwise comparisons (in a choice situation) among n chunks in consciousness; clearly the number n must be limited if the organism is to make a choice within some reasonable time.

A further elaboration of this theme and important for our later arguments is the suggestion that the "limited-capacity mechanism may serve an important inhibitory function . . . [by] giving priority to a particular pathway . . . ."[40] Similarly, in the execution of action, attention is restricted to the central aspects of action selection and execution.[41] The limitation of capacity prevents other structures and schemas from competing overtly with the selected mechanism.

There are occasions and stimuli that demand conscious capacity and construction almost automatically. Among these are intense stimuli and internal physiological events such as intense sympathetic nervous system activity. Whenever such events claim and preoccupy some part of the limited capacity system, other cognitive functions suffer, i.e., they are displaced from conscious processing and problem solving activities are impaired. Particularly in the case of the interruption or

---

[39] Dempster (1981).

[40] Posner and Snyder (1975).

[41] Shallice (1972) and Norman and Shallice (1980).

failure of ongoing conscious and unconscious thought or action, the resultant visceral responses also require conscious representation and interfere even more severely with ongoing conscious activity.[42]

The most ubiquitous of the events that preempt conscious construction is the experience we call "pain." It too follows the general pattern. Pain, despite its insistence, is subject to competition with other events for limited conscious capacity; it can be gated, swamped, suppressed.[43] Pain also comes with additional information; we usually know "where it hurts." In contrast to intense external stimuli, where the source is not always immediately available together with the awareness of the intense event, pain is constructed together with its address. We know at least two things about it--that and where. And it is, of course, highly adaptive to know the "where" if we are to repair the situation that produced the pain. While not conclusive to the argument made here, it would be instructive to know whether newborn infants can localize pain or whether they need to learn that particular conjunction.

The question arises whether we are really "conscious" of five or six discrete events. The arguments for a constructive view of consciousness seem to counsel against such a view. I argued in the previous section that only one view, one conscious construction, of a particular event is possible at any one time and that such a construction responds to intentions and tasks of the moment. If we consider consciousness as an integrated construction of the available evidence, a construction that seems to be phenomenally "whole," then it is more likely that the limitation to a certain number of items or objects or events or chunks refers to the limitation of these elements *within and by* the structures that determine the holistic conscious experience. The schema or schemas that are represented in the conscious construction are necessarily restricted to a certain number of features or relations. Cognitive "chunks" (organized clusters of knowledge) operate as units of such constructed experience. However, only a limited number of such chunks, themselves part of an organized whole, make up part of the current conscious experience. For example, as I look out my window, I am aware of the presence of trees and roads and people, a limited number of individual organized schemas that make up "the view." I may switch my attention--reconstruct my conscious experience--to focus on one of these events and note that some of the people are on bicycles, others walk, some are male, some female. Switching attention (consciousness) again, I see a friend and note that he is limping, carrying a briefcase, and talking with a person walking next to him. At that

---

[42] See Mandler (1979b) for a review.

[43] See, for example, Melzack (1973).

point, the trees, the people on bicycles, etc. are not part of my current consciousness any more. In each case, a new experiential whole enters the conscious state and consists itself of new and different organized chunks.

The organized (and limited) nature of consciousness is illustrated by the fact that one is never conscious of some half dozen totally unrelated things. In the local park I may be conscious of four children playing hopscotch, or of children and parents interacting, or of some people playing chess; but a conscious content of a child, a chessplayer, a father, and a carriage is unlikely (unless of course they form their own meaningful scenario).

In arguing that the limited capacity of consciousness is represented by the number of events that can be organized within a single constructed conscious experience, I respond to the intuitively appealing notion that we are both aware of some unitary "scene" and have available within it a limited number of constituent chunks.[44]

The construction of individual chunks is consistent with the cognitive mechanisms embodied in the distinction between integrative and elaborative processing.[45] Integration refers to the process whereby the elements of a structure (schema) become more strongly related to each other, the structure itself develops its own unique constituents, and the relations among its elements become stable. This process produces organized chunks of knowledge that act as single units, are stored and retrieved as units, and may themselves become elements or features of a larger cognitive structure. Elaboration, on the other hand, refers to the establishment of relationships among structures, the kind of network of relations that is basic to the notion of structural meaning. The relations of a unit of knowledge to other such units determine its meaning and its function in memorial storage and retrieval.[46] The process of elaboration among well-integrated chunks will in turn integrate and define a larger accretion that may itself function as a separate and bounded unit.

Most of the evidence on both the size and the character of the limited capacity of consciousness derives from the notion of mental chunks and the limitation of such chunks. The basic limit of the organizing system is set at about 5 or 6 units, where a unit is a package or chunk

---

[44] I have discussed elsewhere (1984b) the manner in which these momentary conscious states construct the phenomenal continuity and flow of consciousness.

[45] Mandler (1979a, 1980).

[46] See Craik and Tulving (1975), Mandler (1967a, 1982).

of information that may itself be an organized "package."[47] We have shown that access to stored materials is determined both in quantity and access time by the organization of the target material and that categories of about size 5 are the optimal size for both storage and retrieval.[48] Similarly, the recall of organized material is constrained both by the number of things that can be recalled and by the relation among those events. If we look at the free production of materials stored in memory, such as natural categories, we also see the limitation in number AND the constraint of relatedness operating.[49]

I indicated earlier that consciousness may be a necessary accompaniment of encoding into and retrieval from long-term storage. What is usually considered to be recall is deliberate; it is usually conscious, and it involves a search process.[50] What is finally constructed in consciousness is some product of the search process that is consonant with the recall target as described by task, cues, and instructions. In short, we do not recall telephone numbers when trying to remember items on a shopping lists. Recall contrasts with some instances of recognition (when sheer familiarity is accessed) and those cases of reminding when direct access to some memorial content is provided. Clearly, a limitation of capacity is operating in the encoding and retrieval of memorial material. What the available data indicate is that organized groups with no more than about 5 members are retrieved from larger conceptual categories. In retrieving our knowledge of natural categories, we seem to retrieve a small organized chunk that is identified by some theme or concept. The phenomenal experience that accompanies these retrievals also seems to specify a conceptual group and its momentarily limited number of instances. In general, the limitation of consciousness is a function of the number of objects/events that can be accommodated by some unitary organizing principle, whether the objects are words, series of digits, or more complex chunks.

The phenomenon of subitizing, i.e., the rapid, confident, and accurate report of the numerosity of arrays of elements presented for very

---

[47] Miller (1956).

[48] Mandler (1975b).

[49] Mandler and Graesser (1975), Graesser and Mandler (1978).

[50] But see Chapter 4, and the discussion of reminding.

brief exposures,[51] has long been a mainstay in the definition of the limited capacity phenomenon. We have shown in a series of experiments[52] that random collections of dots can be held in consciousness and "counted." The subitizing phenomenon reflects the size limitation of consciousness, as well as the organizational principle. In this case, what organizes the perception of numerosity is the spatiotemporal belongingness of an array of dots. In fact, people are able to appreciate the cognitive clarity of such small arrays of up to 6 objects; they know when they can easily and accurately account for their numerosity.

THE ADAPTIVE FUNCTIONS OF CONSCIOUSNESS

There are many senses of the notion of adaptation, the most widely used one being the adaptive consequence of evolutionary processes. However, the consequences of evolutionary processes are not necessarily adaptive, nor are adaptive functions of an organism necessarily the consequences of selective evolutionary processes focused on the structure or function in question. Utility and universality alone do not argue for evolutionary selection. Just consider that human beings who write universally use their hands, but nobody would argue that evolutionary processes have selected the human hand for its writing utility. Furthermore, the evolution of complex functions is typically the result of the evolution of a wide variety of, sometimes entirely unrelated, functions and structures. Consciousness is probably one such complex function. No single event in our evolutionary history is likely to have resulted in all the aspects of consciousness discussed here. The brief discussion to follow implies no claims about behavioral evolution. It extends the discussion of the uses and functions of consciousness by focusing on those aspects that are, on the average, likely to have made us better suited for the world in which we live and for the events with which we have to cope.

---

[51] Baptized and explored by Kaufman, Lord, Reese, and Volkmann (1949).

[52] Mandler and Shebo (1982).

1. As discussed earlier, the most widely addressed function of consciousness is its role in choice and the selection of action systems. This function permits the organism more complex considerations of action-outcome contingencies that alter the probability of one or another set of actions. It also permits the consideration of possible actions that the organism has never before performed, thus eliminating the overt testing of possible harmful alternatives.[53]

Consciousness makes possible the modification and interrogation of long-range plans as well as of immediate-action alternatives. In the hierarchy of actions and plans, this makes it possible to organize disparate action systems in the service of a higher plan. For example, in planning to drive to some new destination, we might consider subsets of the route; or, in devising a new recipe, the creative chef considers the interactions of several known culinary achievements. Within the same realm, consciousness makes it possible to retrieve and consider modifications in long-range planning activities. These, in turn, might be modified in light of other evidence, either from the immediate environment or from long-term storage.

2. In considering actions and plans, consciousness participates in retrieval from long-term memory, even though the retrieval mechanisms themselves are not conscious. Thus, frequently, although not always, the retrieval of information from long-term storage is initiated by relatively simple commands. These may be simple instructions like, "What is his name?" or "Where did I read about that?" or more complex instructions like, "What is the relation between this situation and previous ones I have encountered?" Answers seem to be just as simple as these questions appear to be. The actual, and complex, retrieval process is "hidden." Such rapid access to stored information illustrates the adaptive use of consciousness in making complex processes more easily accessible.

3. Current states of the world, as well as thoughts and actions, are represented in consciousness and can make use of available structures to construct storable representations for later reference and use. Many investigators have suggested that these encodings of experience always take place in the conscious state. Processes such as mnemonic devices and other strategies for preserving experiences for later reference apparently require the intervention of conscious structures.

---

[53] Mandler and Kessen (1974).

In the social process, prior problem solutions and other memories may be brought into the conscious state and, together with an adequate system of communication, such as human language, generate the benefits of cooperative social efforts. Other members of the species may receive solutions to problems, thus saving time, if nothing else; they may be apprised of unsuccessful alternatives or may, more generally, participate in the cultural inheritance of the group. Such social problem solving and remembering require selection and comparison among alternatives retrieved from long-term storage, all of which apparently takes place in consciousness. Given the often abstract and general nature of conscious contents, the cultural transmission from conscious construction to verbal communication may in fact be extremely efficient. Cultural knowledge can be transmitted and new insights made socially available by the use of general instructions and conclusions, instead of piecemeal communication of detailed skills and minute serial instructions. Just imagine how the mundane matter of teaching somebody how drive a car or make an omelet would be complicated if we could not communicate first our general sense of "how to do it." Without further elaboration, it is obvious that the transaction described here illustrate the intricate relationship between consciousness and language.

We note that both general information and specific sensory inputs may be stored. The re-presentation at some future time makes possible decision processes that depend on comparisons between current and past events and on the retrieval of relevant or irrelevant information for current problem solving.

4. We have already seen that consciousness provides a "troubleshooting" function for structures normally not represented in consciousness. There are many systems that cannot be brought into consciousness; most systems that analyze the environment in the first place probably have that characteristic. In most of these cases, only the product of cognitive and mental activities is available to consciousness. In contrast, many systems are generated and built with the cooperation of conscious processes but later become nonconscious or automatic. The latter systems apparently may be brought into consciousness, particularly when they are defective in their particular function.[54] We all have had experiences of automatically driving a car, typing a letter, or even participating in a cocktail party conversation, and of being suddenly brought up short by some failure such as a defective brake, a stuck key, or a "You aren't listening to me." At that time the particular representations of action and memories involved are brought into play in consciousness, and repair work gets under way. The adaptive

---

[54] See also Vygotsky (1962).

advantage of acting automatically when things go smoothly, but being able to act deliberately when they do not, may therefore also be ascribed to the conscious process.

Many of these functions permit us to react reflectively instead of automatically, a distinction that has frequently been made between human and lower animals. All of them permit more adaptive transactions between the organism and its environment.

IMAGERY AND CONSCIOUSNESS

One of the most ubiquitous aspects of common consciousness is our ability to engage in conscious imagery. Imagery can be mundane or spectacular; it can occur without special effort or be the result of rather intense effort. It also occurs in a variety of sensory modalities. However, both common and psychological usage have shown occasional tendencies to use the term "image" to refer exclusively to visual imagery. This exclusive use of "image" is due in part to the mishap that befell the German word "Vorstellung" in its translation across the Atlantic around the turn of the century. In particular, it led to a sometime misunderstanding of the notion of "imageless thought." The report that associative and judgmental processes at times proceeded without intervening conscious contents was crucial for the development of experimental psychology.[55] But the "images" that were missing were auditory or visual or kinesthetic, replaced by nothing or by contentless conscious experiences *(Bewusstseinslagen)*. In other words, the better translation might have been to employ the actual usage, i.e., to talk about "thought without conscious contents." For the Würzburgers (and most psychologists) any identifiable conscious content was a "Vorstellung", i.e., an image; only the modalities and occasions of occurrence changed. But, if all conscious contents qualify as images or "Vorstellungen", what is a psychology of imagery about? It is a psychology of conscious processes. In addition, when we are dealing with images we are often concerned their effect on other (conscious and unconscious) processes and actions. The study of these specific conscious processes (for example, visual imagery) and their effect is of interest in itself, but still part of a general study of the psychology of consciousness. The generality of such a use of "image" becomes even more apparent when we consider a definition of imagery.

---

[55] For an account of the "discovery" of imageless thought at Würzburg in the early years of the 20th century see Mandler and Mandler (1964).

There are essentially two very distinct aspects of the term "image." Stephen Kosslyn's definition includes them both when he notes that "an image is a representation in the mind that gives rise to the experience of 'seeing' in the absence of the appropriate visual stimulation from the eyes."[56] Kosslyn restricts himself here to visual images. However, the definition applies *pari passu* to the other senses as well; all that needs to be done is to replace "seeing, visual, and eyes" with "hearing, auditory, ears," "smelling, olefactory, nose," or "feeling, visceral, autonomic nervous system." In any case, we apparently are talking about

1. a mental representation, and

2. the phenomenal conscious experience of an image that is constructed out of that representation.

How is that definition different from the definition of any other conscious content? The main difference is that some conscious experiences are constructed in the presence of direct activation from the event in question, whereas in the "image" case the event does not provide immediate activation. But note that such lack of direct activation from sensory stimulation is not restricted to visual or kinesthetic or auditory imagery; the lack also occurs during many of our reveries, whether problem directed or not. If we assume that imagery and "real" conscious percepts access the same underlying representation, one of the differences between the two is the clarity, distinctiveness, and intensity of the conscious experience. In the case of images, the representation is weakly activated, by other related structures or more generally by some conceptual top-down process; we may image a specific event or object simply by being asked to do so or because it fits a scenario in a particular imagined scene, or a dream. In the case of conscious percepts, the activation of the representation is direct; there is evidence from the environment that speaks directly to the representation. In short, we can treat imagery as a special case of the problem of conscious construction.

Imagery generates conscious constructions in the absence of specific environmental evidence. The uses of imagery are therefore part of the uses of consciousness in general; imagery adds the advantage that the effects of consciousness can be made available free of contextual constraints. Imagery makes possible the construction of mental models and the mental simulation of past (and future) situations.

---

[56] Kosslyn (1983, p.29) .

CONSEQUENCES OF CONSCIOUSNESS

I mentioned earlier that one of the arguments against the causal efficacy of conscious states is that they usually occur *after* the event with which they are supposedly causally connected. The basis of that argument is found in the persisting speculations about mind-body relations, and specifically how it is that nonpalpable conscious (mental) states could cause physical (body) events. I do not intend to elaborate on the mind-body problem, but rather to suggest that conscious states have effects on *subsequent* mental events and human (physical) actions.

Our discussion of the functions and processes of consciousness leads to a number of generalizations, which, together with some simple assumptions, suggest the following summary and lead to an important additional adaptive function for momentary consciousness:

First, consciousness is limited in capacity and it is constructed so as to respond to the situational and intentional imperatives of the moment.

Second, observable thoughts and actions are to be explained in terms of unconscious representations and processes.

Third, the underlying representations are subject to activations, both by external events and by internal (conceptual) processes.

Fourth, activated structures (such as schemas) are necessary for the eventual occurrence of observable thought and actions. Current models of schema theory and the more sophisticated, but compatible, models of parallel distributed processes are all based on these assumptions.

I add to these a fifth assumption, namely, that *events represented in consciousness also activate relevant underlying structures.*

The implication of the fourth assumption is that activation is necessary for structures to become incorporated into conscious states in the first place. The additional assumption expands this notion and states that the possible alternatives, choices, and competing hypotheses that have been represented in consciousness will receive additional activation and thus will be enhanced.[57] Given the capacity limitation of consciousness combined with the intentional selection of conscious states, very few preconscious candidates for actions and thoughts will achieve this additional, consciousness-mediated activation.[58] As a result, thought and action on subsequent occasions will make use of those preconscious structures that are selected as most responsive to current demands and intentions. Whatever structures are used for a current conscious construction will receive additional activation, and they will have been those selected as most relevant to current concerns. In contrast, alternatives that were candidates for conscious thought of action but were not selected will be relegated to a relatively lower probability of selection on subsequent occasions.

The evidence for this general effect is derived from the vast amount of current research showing that sheer activation and its frequency affect subsequent accessibility for thought and action, whether in the area of perceptual priming, recognition memory, preserved amnesic functions, or decision making.[59] The present proposal extends such activations from external evidence to internally generated events and, in particular, the momentary states of consciousness constructed to satisfy internal and external demands. Thus, just as reading a sentence produces activation of the underlying schemas, so does (conscious) thinking of that sentence or its gist activate relevant structures. In the former case, what is activated depends on what the world presents to us; in the latter the activation is determined and limited by the conscious construction.

This hypothesis of selective and limited activation of situationally relevant structures requires no homunculus-like function for consciousness in which some independent agency controls, selects, and directs thoughts and actions that have been made available in consciousness. Given an appropriate database, it should be possible to simulate this particular function of consciousness without an appeal to an independent decision-making agency.

---

[57] Note that these activations are *in addition* to the usual flow of activation that takes place during unconscious processing (see, for example, McClelland and Rumelhart, 1981).

[58] Posner and Snyder's (1975) hypothesis that conscious states preempt pathways by the inhibition of competing possibilities may in part be related to the assumption that such pathways are more available because of preferential additional activation.

[59] Graf, Squire, and Mandler (1984), Jacoby and Dallas (1981), Mandler (1979a, 1980), McClelland and Rumelhart (1981), Meyer and Schvaneveldt (1976), Tversky and Kahneman (1973). And see John Anderson's work for a more theoretical account (e.g., Anderson, 1983).

The proposal can easily be expanded to account for some of the phenomena of human problem solving. I assume that activation is necessary but not sufficient for conscious construction and that activation depends in part on prior conscious constructions. The search for problem solutions and the search for memorial targets (as in recall) typically have a conscious counterpart, frequently expressed in introspective protocols. What appear in consciousness in these tasks are exactly those points in the course of the search when steps toward the solution have been taken and a choice point has been reached at which the immediate next steps are not obvious. At that point the current state of world is reflected in consciousness. That state reflects the progress toward the goal as well as some of the possible steps that could be taken next. A conscious state is constructed that responds to those aspects of the current search that *do* (partially and often inadequately) respond to the goal of the search. Consciousness at these points truly depicts waystations toward solutions and serves to restrict and focus subsequent pathways by selectively activating those that are currently within the conscious construction. For example, as I try to remember when and with whom I undertook a particular unpublished experimental study, I recall the names of some students and colleagues who were interested in that problem. None of the names seem to satisfy the goal of my search, but I next recall that one of these people had a passing interest in the particular experiment I am trying to place. I then recall that this person had an office mate whose name escapes me for the moment, and I try to reconstruct the physical layout of our labs and offices. I recover an image of that office mate, then remember her name, and immediately remember that, while not directly involved in the conceptual problem, she had offered to conduct the experiment with me. The conscious waystations and how they might have redistributed structural activations appear in this account. Whenever I reached an impasse, conscious contents focused on the dilemma and provided new activations that led to new conscious states, and so forth until a solution was reached. For example, one waystation included a representation of a selected set of students and colleagues; another one appeared next as result of the activation of this set together with the prior activation of the "particular experiment" and produced a narrower conscious focus of possible candidates. Those preconscious structures that construct consciousness at the time of impasse, delay, or interruption receive additional activation, as do those still unconscious structures linked with them. The result is a directional flow of activation that would not have happened without the extra boost derived from the conscious state.

Research on problem solving that focuses on the conscious aspects of mental products[60] may have to consider that what is reportable is the product of more fundamental processes. In addition, these underlying processes are themselves activated by the contents of the conscious states that are used as the primary evidence of the solution process. In that sense introspective statements are the tip of the iceberg, waystations that themselves need to be seen as having a causal role.

Another phenomenon that argues for the representation of conscious contents is our ability to "think about" previous conscious contents; we can be aware of our awareness. There is anecdotal as well as experimental evidence that we are sometimes confused between events that "actually" happened and those that we merely imagined, i.e., events that were present in consciousness but not in the surrounds. Clearly the latter must have been stored in a manner similar to the way "actual" events are stored.[61] It has been argued that this awareness of awareness (self-awareness) is in principle indefinitely self-recursive, that is, that we can perceive a lion, be aware that we are perceiving a lion, be conscious of our awareness of perceiving a lion, and so forth *ad infinitum*.[62] In fact, I have never been able to detect any such extensive recursion in myself, nor has anybody else to my knowledge. We can certainly be aware of somebody (even ourselves) asserting the recursion, but observing it is another matter.[63] The recursiveness *in consciousness* ends after two or three steps, that is, within the structural limit of conscious organization.

The positive feedback that consciousness provides for activated and constructed mental contents is, of course, not limited to problem-solving situations. It is, for example, evident in the course of self-instructions. We frequently keep reminding ourselves (consciously) of tasks to be performed, actions to be undertaken. "Thinking about" these future obligations makes it more likely that we will remember to undertake them when the appropriate time arrives. Thus, self-directed comments, such as, "I must remember to write to Mary" or "I shouldn't

---

[60] For example, Newell and Simon (1972).

[61] R.E. Anderson (1984), Johnson and Raye (1981).

[62] For example, by Johnson-Laird (1983).

[63] Just because we can talk about infinite recursions does not imply that we can engage in it any more than we are able jump over the Eiffel tower just because we can talk about (imagine) it.

forget to pick up some bread on the way home," make remembering more likely and forgetting less likely. Such self-reminding keeps the relevant information highly activated, ready to be brought into consciousness when the appropriate situation for execution appears.[64] Self-directed comments can, of course, be deleterious as well as helpful. The reoccurrence of obsessive thoughts is a pathological example, but everyday "obsessions" are the more usual ones. Our conscious constructions may end up in a loop of recurring thoughts that preempt limited capacity and often prevent more constructive and situationally relevant "thinking." One example is trying to remember a name and getting stuck with an obviously erroneous target that keeps interfering with more fruitful attempts at retrieval. The usual advice to stop thinking about the problem, because it will "come to us" later, appeals to an attempt to let the activation of the "error" return to lower levels before attempting the retrieval once again. Another example of the deleterious effects of haphazard activation is represented in the likelihood of consciousness being captured by a mundane occurrence. Thus, as we drive home, planning to pick up that loaf of bread, conscious preoccupation with a recent telephone call may capture conscious contents to the exclusion of other, now less activated, candidates for conscious construction, such as the intent to stop at the store. Or, planning to go to the kitchen to turn off the stove, we may be "captured" by a more highly activated and immediate conscious content of a telephone call. The "kitchen-going" intention loses out unless we refresh its activation by reminding ourselves, while on the phone, about the intended task. Too often, we fail to keep that activation strong enough and the plan in mind--and our dinner is burned.

The additional function of consciousness as outlined here is generally conservative in that it underlines and reactivates those mental contents that are currently used in conscious constructions and are apparently the immediately most important and useful ones. It also encompasses the observation that under conditions of stress people tend to repeat previously unsuccessful attempts at problem solution.[65] Despite this unadaptive consequence, a reasonable argument can be made that it is frequently useful for the organism to continue to do what apparently is successful and appears to be most appropriate. However, as a corollary of this mechanism, events that are totally disruptive and inappropriate to the current context should have a quite different function. There is

---

[64] This kind of "rehearsal" needs to be distinguished from another kind that is designed merely to keep some information in a current conscious state. The latter is encountered when we repeat a new telephone number in the short period between looking it up and dialing.

[65] See Mandler (1979b).

no obvious conscious construction that can be adopted when both the currently dominant action tendencies and their possible alternatives are evidently inadequate. It is at this point that new structures, some of which previously may have been at some relatively weakly activated level, will be called into service. I discuss the emotional (particularly autonomic) consequences of such interruptions and discrepancies in Chapter 4. What I argue here is that in addition to these consequences there are purely mental/cognitive ones. When current activations from the environment, the causes of the disruption, do not readily find an appropriate structure that accommodates to their characteristics, then spreading activation will eventually find some alternative structures that provide some support for the new evidence generated by the world.

Novel ways of structuring the world can be found in a variety of situations, some of which are often bizarre or incongruous, whether in science or in science fiction. Such new constructions are also found in dreams, which are not under the control of environmental regularities. I have argued elsewhere[66] that in dreams the daily residual activation will, in the absence of any schematic direction from the environment, find other higher order structures that can accommodate them--and sometimes in unexpected and bizarre combinations.

The ability to create interruptions, new ways of seeing the world out of joint, seems to be necessary for scientific as well as aesthetic creations. An interesting example is found in the French psychoanalyst Jacques Lacan's use of the totally unexpected shortening and interruption of his sessions with clients. One participant reports his personal experience with one of Lacan's unexpected short sessions: "The ending of the session, unexpected and unwanted, was like a rude awakening, like being torn out of a dream by a loud alarm. (One patient likened it to *coitus interruptus*)." These short sessions seem to facilitate access to the unconscious and "[t]he combined pressure of the shortness of the sessions and the unpredictability of their stops creates a condition that greatly enhances one's tendencies to free-associate . . . ."[67]

---

[66] Mandler (1984b).

[67] Schneiderman (1983).

THE USES OF CONSCIOUSNESS

I now return to the question with which I began this exploration: What advantages does this proposed mechanism confer on the organism it inhabits? What are we able to do with it that we could not do without it? I do not think the additional abilities are either mysterious or overwhelming, but, like many changes to our evolutionary makeup, they increment our more primitive abilities. The proposed mechanism requires no novel mechanism; it just extends the activation process--the result follows automatically. It does create conditions for making internal search processes as efficacious as external ones; we need not scan the world in order to benefit from the various possibilities that surround us. Third, it significantly speeds up decision processes and problem solving by adding information that might otherwise have to be obtained rather laboriously from the external world.

The alternative to self-activation via consciousness requires additional searches, either of the environment or of stored information. Organisms not endowed with this conscious feedback mechanism or not yet able to take advantage of it are clearly more dependent on environmental information and very often on trial and error behavior. Infants, who cannot recall in the sense used here, show such dependence;[68] and, without entering into speculations about infant consciousness, it can be argued within the present context that neither the relevant action and event schemas nor the higher order task and intentional structures are available to the newborn.[69] Lower animals develop strategies of increasing the activation of current alternatives in their attempt to solve problems. For example, some animals display so called vicarious trial and error (VTE) behavior at choice points.[70] VTEs consist of visual sampling of possible choices, sometimes including short forays to one side or the other before a choice occurs. VTEs can be seen as precursors of imagery (and consciousness), maximizing data input in the absence of representation in consciousness. Humans too are known to use similar strategies when unable to generate reasonable hypotheses about the current state of the world.

---

[68] See, for example, Piaget (1970).

[69] See J.M. Mandler (1984a).

[70] Muenzinger (1938).

The mechanisms that select the relevant and important from the many potential sources of information in the environment are central to an organism's ability to deal with its world. Momentary states of consciousness are the final step in the reduction of information that floods the organism. Having arrived at a view of mental representation that invokes an efficient and economical system of parallel distributed processes, we can now invoke consciousness to provide us with a slow, restricted, and serial processing state. For example, when decisions need to be restricted to few candidates or when problem solving reaches a stalemate, consciousness provides a deliberate stage for further appropriate action. States of consciousness not only reduce the flow of information to manageable proportions, but also make sense out of what is available and make subsequent actions more adaptive.

Most if not all our knowledge and previous experience is stored (available, recorded) in structures that are both vast and differentially accessible. Some distinction needs to be made between that information and what is currently being used, worked on, and accessed. It is to a large part that function that is being exercised by consciousness. If one were aware (conscious) of *everything one knows,* or even of everything that is relevant (closely related to) some current experience, one would be swamped with information and unable to act. Thus the distinction needs to be made; and, in the course of the evolution of the mind, the distinction emerged in the human species as that between conscious and unconscious mental contents, as it possibly developed also in other complex animals faced with the same dilemma.

It is possible that other useful functions of consciousness emerged as a consequence of the emergence of consciousness, and not as a direct selective adaptation. In particular, the relation of thought and language may well have been such a later development, in part because of the usefulness of language for summarizing and capsulating event and thoughts. It is certainly the case that the interplay between human conscious thought and language has overwhelmed our view of both of them, often asserting that one could not exist without the other.[71]

One of the adaptive functions of consciousness, though not necessarily a result of specific natural selection, is the function of consciousness that chunks and abstracts knowledge into serviceable units for the social communication of knowledge.

---

[71] Révész (1954), Vygotsky (1962).

It permits the communicator to restrict the message to its salient aspects, and it also makes easier the reception of a limited rather than overinclusive "message." In addition, it permits the participants in social communication (and the transmission of culture) to construct reasonably concise and common mental models of social knowledge.[72]

ATTENTION

Since notions of consciousness and attention have frequently been coextensive in recent cognitive speculations, we do need to consider the function of attentional processes in the scheme of things. The common usage frequently coalesces attention, analytic processes, and consciousness. It is said, for example, that one attends to the theme of a musical composition, to the message in a speech, to the colors in a painting. In contrast, the attention concept need claim only that one focuses on the spatiotemporal source of the music, the speech, or the painting, that is, on general locations and occasions in one's environment.

Most current theories of attention fall into two broad classes: early-selection theories and late-selection theories. Early-selection theories claim that top-down processes, sometimes called attentional mechanisms, select only parts of the perceptual continuum and inhibit or filter (exclude) others.[73] Late-selection theories admit all the available evidence to analytic, parallel (activational) processes and then select relevant aspects of the available unconscious evidence.[74] In both kinds of theories, there is frequently some implication that the selection process involves the use (construction) of a conscious state.

Alternatively, one may define attention as being independent of consciousness and restrict it to the potential intake of formation. Attention is the process whereby a specific part of the space-time continuum is automatically made available for further processing. As a result, the information potentially available in the spatiotemporal section that is scanned is accessible to all relevant analytic processes. Typically, conceptual (top-down) processes will select the analyses to be per-

---

[72] Donald Griffin (1984) has suggested that the conditions of consciousness ("thinking") apply also to nonhuman animals. He argues that concepts and generalizations are needed to stand in for detailed specifications, that thinking and decisions need to be relatively rapid, and that the behavior of animals indicates the exercise of consciousness.

[73] Broadbent (1958) and Treisman (1964, 1969).

[74] Deutsch and Deutsch (1963) and Shiffrin and Schneider (1977).

formed. Under some circumstances the nature of the information scanned may command analytic processes, as, for example, in the "attention" paid to a loud noise or bright light. As a result of spatiotemporal attention and the subsequent activation of selected cognitive representations, the structures (schemas) activated by these two processes will be available for the construction of the unified phenomenal experience. When the part of the spatiotemporal continuum that is selected by attention is very narrow and when the consequent activated schemas are determined primarily by the information scanned and by a (small) number of relevant schemas, the conscious contents will be determined and generally invariant from situation to situation and person to person (e.g., in the psychophysical experiment or by the demands of a loud noise or of a familiar word).

There is no deliberate or "top down" selection in this view of attention, except for the primitive process that includes or excludes parts of the spatiotemporal flux. Selection phenomena and attentional priorities are determined at the next level of analysis and beyond, after the mere intake of the "physical" information from the spatiotemporal flux has taken place. Parallel (late selection) or serial (early selection) processing can then proceed on the given unanalyzed information, followed in most instances by conscious construction. For example, the request to "look for a red object in this room" does *not* involve a peripheral looking for red objects; what does happen is that the whole room becomes the domain of the spatiotemporal continuum that is scanned. Independently of this directive process, another top-down process will then select the evidence that fits the "red" criterion. Relevant evidence on this purely spatiotemporal selection by attentive processes has been developed in recent work on the "size" of the attentional spotlight.[75] In a sense, this is a combination of the early- and late-selection views. However, the "early" selection advocated here is neutral with respect to conceptual or semantic features. Most of the work that is appealed to by the commonsense notion of attention is done by late-selection mechanisms.

In summary, then, we can recast "early" and "late" models of attention, not as competitive explanations of the same phenomenon, but as distinct stages and modes. Each of these "stages" addresses a different set of phenomena, and alltogether these various processes constitute the general concept of "attention." I have already noted that "attention" canot be used as coextensive with consciousness. The additional arguments presented above speak to the steps at which information is "gathered" and to the possible conscious constructions that result from the intitial activations. The selective nature of

---

[75] LaBerge (1983).

constructive consciousness uses the information most appropriate to the current task and goals. Such construction may be early or late; it may use serial or parallel processes. The concept of attention can then be reserved for the initial step in the information flow where specific spatiotemporal targets become the objects for further processing. A similar position has been taken by Daniel Kahneman and Anne Treisman, who have argued that "attention is assigned to objects, or to the locations that objects occupy, rather than to nodes in long-term memory."[76]

CONSCIOUSNESS AND PSYCHOANALYTIC THEORY

No discussion of consciousness can be concluded without making contact with the contribution of Sigmund Freud, who more than any other single individual is responsible for our dawning understanding of both the conscious and the unconscious. There is very little in the way of direct descent from Freud to contemporary cognitive theories, whose ancestry derives from Kant, Gestalt psychology, Bartlett, and Piaget on the one hand and Helmholtz, sensory psychology and mathematical psychology on the other. However, the attempt at a principled mentalism, a rejection of reductionism, and a theoretical understanding of the structures and representations that underlie human thought and action unites all of these trends with Freud.

At the end of the century, the historical push for a theoretical (non-physiological) psychology was exemplified in the first instance by Freud and a little later by the Würzburgers, who also realized that there was more to human thought than what is represented in consciousness. To read Freud primarily as a biologist[77] misreads the historical importance of his *shift* from physiological to psychological explanation.

My main concern is with Freud circa 1900, particularly with the dream book, and more specifically with the theory spelled out in Chapter 7 of the TRAUMDEUTUNG.[78] With that work, Freud reacted to the major imperatives of the social, intellectual, and scientific forces that shaped the fin de siècle. Unfortunately, he rarely returned to the early theoretical themes of the mechanisms of the unconscious, preconscious, and conscious. He became more enmeshed in theoretical attempts that were a reflection of personal and social concerns identified

---

[76] Kahneman and Treisman (1984).

[77] Sulloway (1979).

[78] Freud (1900).

with his society and class. The forces of Eros and Thanatos raged in the context of a nuclear family marked by the competitive characteristics of middle class Western industrial society. In the brief remarks to follow I confine myself to affinities between cognitive theory and Freud's distinction among the unconscious, the preconscious, and the conscious.

It is in the context of schema theory and consciousness that similarities between current work and Freud's formulations become apparent. The partition among unconscious schemas, activated ones, and those used in the construction of consciousness is essentially the same as Freud's among conscious, preconscious and unconscious states. For Freud too, unconscious contents must pass through the preconscious stage before reaching consciousness. For example, he says that preconscious processes can enter into consciousness "without further impediment," and unconscious contents have "no access to consciousness *except via the preconscious.*"[79]

Freud was one of the theorists of consciousness whom Marcel described as advocates of the *identity assumption.*[80] However, Freud's view is closer to a constructivist position when he talks about conscious contents hiding underlying motives that may appear in some altered form. In principle, there is no difference between high order schemas that direct what is useful and appropriate in restaurants and in decorators' offices and those abstract schemas that determine our consciousness when we think of parents, lovers, and childhood preoccupations. Both require constructions that make use of thematic schemas as well as current concerns.

Thematic schemas are obviously close relations of the childhood complexes and preoccupations that Freud assigned first to his patients and eventually to us all. A conception of the flexibility of schematic growth and organization is, however, a step in a more positive direction; it permits us to see a wide variety of possible adult themes (or complexes) that are restricted only by the development that the culture and society dictate. When those experiences can easily be described with little variability among members of the cultural group, then similar developments of personality and motivations will occur. However, these themes will change as society and its fashions change with regard to child rearing, attitudes toward cultural institutions and structures, and real world contingencies.

---

[79] Freud (1900).

[80] Marcel (1983b).

Themes and schemas are often inaccessible. They may not be subject to activation at all, even though they do form part of the unconscious structures; they do not enter the preconscious. Alternatively, they may be activated (preconscious) but not available for conscious construction. This distinction raises interesting questions about the problem of repression. For example, if thinking about (bringing to consciousness) a topic is blocked and some less threatening and related topic is brought to consciousness instead, do we really know much about the detailed mechanism involved? For example, consider two related concepts X and Y, where X is repressed because it may lead to conflict and negative affect, but Y is the "safe" symbolic substitute, the displacement. Is X repressed and not activated, while Y is activated and available for conscious construction? Or, are both X and Y activated and then X is blocked from being brought into consciousness? Or are both kinds of mechanism possible? If so, when do they make their appearance? More generally, what is the specific blocking mechanism in repression?

Finally, the parallel between a "cognitive" account of dreams and Freud's is obvious. The former has of course been influenced and directed by the Freudian legacy, but it also flows freely from cognitive theory itself. In fact, the general notion of the effect of prior activations on subsequent experience has been extensively investigated by cognitive psychologists who could profitably turn their efforts to the study of residual activations that are effective in dreams.

CHAPTER 4

Past and Future Directions

A small, and sometimes speculative, book such as this cannot possibly cover all the active areas currently considered to be "cognitive." If, as I suggested in Chapter 1, cognitive psychology is not a separate part of psychology but rather the leading edge of mainstream psychology, the problem of coverage becomes even more daunting. As a result, this last chapter will cover some selected topics, and it will focus on two of them--memory and emotion. These two areas represent a mainstay of cognitive psychology (memory) and a topic that is receiving increasing attention (emotion). The choice was, of course, also made because emotion and memory are two aspects of cognitive psychology in which I have a long-standing interest and some competence.

I start with a brief discussion of the hallmark of cognitive psychology--the notion of human information processing. I then turn to the most obvious topic, memory, which has dominated cognitive psychology from the beginning. Following another traditional topic that deserves more "cognitive" attention, learning, I turn to a nontraditional one, the problem of emotion and value, which is a central aspect of human functioning that has only recently been attended to by cognitive psychologists.

HUMAN INFORMATION PROCESSING

I indicated in Chapter 1 that human information processing (HIP) was an early characteristic of cognitive psychology and at the same time was incorrectly seen as making testable (falsifiable) assertions. But information processing is not a theory; it is at best a way of talking about certain interesting phenomena. Although it surely is not a unitary theory in any sense of the term, it does define a particular way of doing psychology--or at least it did. The HIP approach in the 1950s and 1960s was the first step from the stimulus-response psychology of the preceding era to contemporary cognitive psychology. HIP replaced Ss and Rs with inputs and outputs, a change in terminology that probably did no more than define a break with the past. But the major change was to replace a concern with the relations among inputs and inputs with the analysis of the chain of events that mediated the input-output relations. Mediational models had appeared in behaviorist theories during the 1940s and 1950s, but they were mixed models that still incorporated the static concepts of habits and response strengths. Information processing required deterministic chains of inferred events. It was that characteristic--of complex theory--that identified information processing then and characterizes cognitive psychology today.

The early processing models were simple box models, postulating undefined steps (designated by arrows in ubiquitous flow charts) that went from uninvestigated states to other such states (designated by boxes in the flow charts). They were uniformly serial models. With the development of cognitive psychology, the concern with simple input-output relations dimmed and the major interest began to center on the nature of the internal inferred mechanisms--the representations and processes. We became interested in the content of the boxes.

If serial processing was one of the landmarks of early information processing approaches, chronometry, the analysis of processing and reaction times, was the other. The notion that the time to access various mental contents and processes could provide important clues to the structure of the mind was first developed 100 years earlier by F.C. Donders.[1] In the current era, representative and pioneering work in this area was done by Michael Posner, Saul Sternberg, and Roger Shepard. The problems addressed were as diverse as determining the difference between physical and conceptual representations, i.e., distinguishing

---

[1] Donders (1862).

access to top down and bottom up information;[2] the scanning of mental contents available after a brief presentation;[3] and the nature of visual representations and their manipulation.[4]

The serial view of mental processing was challenged by two connected developments. First, doubt was cast on the assumption that successive processes in the information processing flow were initiated upon the completion of their predecessors. James McClelland proposed a cascade model in which a particular process passes partial information on to the subsequent and parallel mechanisms before its own work has been completed.[5] The second innovation followed naturally from the first, i.e., that mental processes are not in fact serially organized but may occur in parallel and provide interactive products during such parallel processing. The development of parallel processing notions occurred hand in hand with the promotion of distributed processes (see Chapter 2). Once one considers representation to be distributed rather than locally organized, the idea of parallel processes operating over these representations follows naturally.[6]

The general adoption of a model of parallel information processing did, however, create a new problem. Action and thought are obviously serially organized; how does a parallel system produce serial output? I want to draw attention to one important solution. As I indicated in Chapter 3, conscious constructions are eminently serial, and one of the major characteristics of consciousness is its limited, serial character. Thus, conscious states permit the selection from among parallel activated structures into a the serially organized stream of conscious thought.

---

[2] Posner (1969).

[3] Sternberg (1966).

[4] Shepard and Metzler (1971), Shepard (1978).

[5] McClelland (1979).

[6] See Hinton and Anderson(1981), Rumelhart and McClelland (1985).

MEMORY

Memory is a catchall term, an umbrella category from the common language, that speaks to occasions (but not all of them, such as ongoing perceptual activity) when previously experienced events are represented in some symbolic form or when they affect some current activities. It is NOT a separate faculty or a specific kind of mechanism (not even two, like episodic and semantic), but rather it makes use of a variety of different mechanisms that operate on mental representations. Which of these mechanisms and representations will be used depends on the nature of the task facing the individual and the context in which the task occurs.

Reminding, Recalling, Recognizing: Different Memories?

The concept of memory refers to current conscious constructions about previously experienced events. At least, that is the way it seems to be used in the common language and by most psychologists. Clearly, it does not refer to the effect of all prior experiences that affect current functioning, though the confusion does exist at times when some psychologists talk about contextual effects on perception as being part of, or making use of, (long-term) memory. To the extent that human minds have histories and change over time, all mental activity could be considered to be memorial, and the term loses all useful meaning. Nor are all conscious constructions memorial--the current view out of my window is not, except in the sense just rejected. However, we speak of memory when I remember (am conscious of) an accident I witnessed the last time I looked out the window. We talk about memory when some current conscious construction incorporates some referent to a previously experienced event. Such referents occur, and "memory" is invoked, whether we deliberately recall some event, or are accidentally reminded of it, or recognize an event as having previously occurred in a similar form or context.

Most of so-called memory experiences involve two of the basic processes discussed earlier: activation and conscious construction. Within the constraints of these two domains, memorial events display a multitude of different characteristics, employ a host of strategies, and may be subdivided into a number of categories and different "kinds" of memories. I discuss some of these distinctions, such as short vs. long term and episodic vs. semantic, later. A more pervasive distinction can be made between automatic and nonautomatic access to mental contents.[7]

There is a variety of terms that describe two different kinds of memorial experiences. Usually they fall under the two rubrics of automatic and nonautomatic memories or retrievals. Various kinds of concepts are included within these two classes and they are listed here:

AUTOMATIC	NON-AUTOMATIC
Fast	Slow
Immediate	Mediated
Unconscious	Conscious
Uncontrolled	Controlled
No capacity demand	Capacity demanding
Direct access	Indirect access
Involuntary	Voluntary
Context free	Context dependent

Automatic memories are fast. We are reminded of a previous visit when we enter a restaurant, but the retrieval of what we ordered may take quite a while. In the same sense, the memory of the previous visit is not mediated by some other conscious waystations, although the memory of the specific meal may require mediate waystations, including memory aides such as a copy of the menu. We do not "try" consciously to remember the previous visit. Access is unconscious, the memory popping into mind; whereas remembering the old repast is deliberate and conscious. The latter is controlled by the mediating events; the former is not under conscious control. Access to the memory of the previous visit occurs without any conscious capacity that is used in retrieval, but it is unlikely that we can do much else besides trying to recover the memory when we think of the specific items ordered. In common parlance, the memory of the visit is involuntary; we "voluntarily" try to recover the detailed remembrance. For context dependency, we need a somewhat different example, because the memory of the prior visit is confined to the activations produced by the self-same restaurant. However, context-free memories occur frequently in recognition phenomena, when we see a familiar face, or a painting, or a friend's car. These "recognitions" may occur in any context--in a bus, a gallery, a book, a photograph, or a drawing. However, the specific knowledge of the name of the person, the painter, the make of

---

[7] See, for example, Hasher and Zacks (1979).

the car may be context dependent and require the situation or other surrounding facts that mark the person, painting, or car.

These two classes of memories may be more generally defined as:

1. Relatively fast retrievals that require no conscious processing,
vs.
2. Relatively slow retrievals that require conscious processing.

Automatic retrievals appear to be confined to previously organized, well-bounded, and unitary objects and events, typically involving a single organized schema. Nonautomatic retrievals, on the other hand, typically involve relations among two or more such structures. It should be stressed that these are not two different memory systems. Admittedly there are some mental contents that are accessed exclusively by one or the other of these avenues. For example, the procedure of cutting up the meat on one's plate is automatic and difficult to access consciously, except in the sense of secondary schemas (see Chapter 2). On the other hand, for most people, remembering the name of the 5th President of the United States requires conscious processing (though it might not for some diligent students of American history). However, the same representation of an event may, under different circumstances, be accessed by one or the other of these mechanisms.

The best examples of such differential access is found in a variety of studies of patients with anterograde amnesia. These people cannot recall events or objects recently encountered, but they can sometimes recognize them, and will, under proper circumstances, report them as "coming to mind." The same phenomenon can be demonstrated in nonpatient populations.

Reminding, in Amnesia and Elsewhere

Psychologists are constantly reminded of things to do and think about, without making any deliberate effort to do so. Yet they tend to investigate only deliberate efforts to recover previously experienced events. Why we have studied deliberate memories almost to the exclusion of the nondeliberate ones is another mistery in the sociology of our science. The omission is particularly puzzling, since Hermann Ebbinghaus, in his inauguration of the experimental study of memory, clearly spelled out the difference between these kinds of memories.[8]

To introduce noneffortful remembering, called here "reminding" for short, we turn to a brief look at the performance of amnesic patients who can be reminded but cannot deliberately recall newly experienced events. Patients with anterograde amnesia characteristically show intact premorbid memories, but their ability to acquire new information is severely impaired. The amnesia for new information is incomplete, however. Whereas amnesics are unable to recall a list of words presented to them, they can use information from the list when given the first three letters of each word (e.g., DEF..., or CHA...) with instructions to complete these word-stems to form English words. Elizabeth Warrington and Larry Weiskrantz[9] showed that although amnesic patients are inferior to normal control subjects in the recall task, they are equal to normals in the completion task. The performance of amnesics is surprising inasmuch as they produce the words but do not remember having studied the list or any list of words.

The same disjunction of performance on recall and completion can be found with college students. The students were given one of two tasks with a list of words: rating words for meaning or counting the vowels that two successive words had in common. Students who were given the vowel task were unable to recall the words, whereas those who rated the meaning of the words were able to recall them. However, when required to complete the word stems, the two groups were indistinguishable. After producing the words on the completion test, the subjects who had been given the vowel task attributed their poor recall of the words to the incidental task that prevented them from "looking at the words."[10] The presentation in the vowel task was sufficient to activate the perceptual aspect of the word so that the vowel group was able to complete the words on the basis of the integrative aspect of their representation. In particular, the appropriate completions, rather than alternate ones, seemed to "come to mind" automatically.

The presentation of a word fragment results in the partial activation of a schema; existing relations among the activated components then bring about their mutual activation, and this activation quickly spreads to the missing components. In terms of the distinction between elaboration and integration discussed in Chapter 2, the completion test

---

[8] Ebbinghaus (1885), see Mandler (1985) for a discussion.

[9] Warrington and Weiskrantz (1970, 1974).

[10] Graf, Mandler, and Haden (1982).

takes advantage of the integrative aspect of a representation.[11] Both in recall and in episodic recognition, retrieval is required, and therefore performance depends on prior elaboration. The completion task, on the other hand, does not require any active search process; its performance can be primarily a function of the words that have become automatically more accessible. Since sheer presentation increases activation/integration, the completion task requires only that the individual give the word that automatically "comes to mind." The residual activation from the prior exposure, together with the re-activation due to the stem cue, will make the presented word a more likely candidate for completing the 3-letter stem than other possible completions.

Those tasks ask people to write the *first words to come to mind* as completions of the first three letters of previously presented words.[12] A comparable pattern of results has been found under similar test conditions in a word identification experiment.[13] These results suggest that the activation/integration of the schema for a word is independent of elaborative (semantic) processing, which may be impaired in amnesics, whereas integration is an automatic process that makes a word more accessible for some time after its presentation. Others have argued that amnesics store new information like normal controls and that their memory deficit is due to a retrieval defect, which could be overcome by providing additional cues for the memory test (as in the completion test). If the deficit were in the storing or encoding phase, then no amount of additional, improved cueing should be effective, the information not having been acquired in the first place. Such an argument assumes that what is stored is a single unidimensional trace and that various kinds of tests of memory are differentially effective in accessing that trace.[14] In contrast, I suggest that different aspects of the representation of an event are accessed in different "tests" of memory. In the case of the completion test, the word stem accesses only the integrated schema of the event and not the elaborated relations between the target word and the context in which it was presented. A similar effect can be observed in recognition, when people can access the "familiarity" of an

---

[11] See also Horowitz and Prytulak (1969) who used "redintegration" to describe this process of filling in the missing components of a recently experienced event.

[12] Graf, Mandler, and Haden (1982), Graf, Squire, and Mandler (1984).

[13] Jacoby and Dallas (1981).

[14] Warrington and Weiskrantz (1970).

event without being able to place the event in context.[15] However, typically both the elaborated and the integrated aspect of the representation of events are accessed in recognition performance, whereas in the case of recall, the elaboration of the schema (its relation to other mental contents) is the primary determinant of the accessibility of the to-be-remembered event. However, the integration of the representation also plays a role in the degree of the distinctiveness of the retrieved event.

I have spent some time on an exploration of memory deficits and their sometime absence in amnesic patients because the distinctions made not only address the selective inability to benefit from recent experiences that is characteristic of amnesic patients,[16] but they also describe one aspect of reminding experiences in everyday life, when things come to mind as result of automatic activation. The selective inability to benefit from recent experiences (anterograde amnesia) is characterized by an impairment in elaborative processing and intact integrative processing. Amnesic patients have no difficulty with a task that requires automatic utilization of some previous integration; they have difficulty in accessing material that depends on recent elaborative encoding. For other people, many events come to mind that may not have been the result of deliberate recall, sometimes even when such deliberate retrieval efforts have failed. The current interest in these distinctions has generated a number of hypotheses, most of which seem consistent with this approach. Thus distinctions between horizontal and vertical associative learning,[17] between procedural and declarative knowledge,[18] and between intentional and incidental processing,[19] all seem to address similar dimensions. However, my interpretation is in contrast to views that have argued that the dissociations involve different memory systems.[20] In general, the memory deficit in anterograde amnesia, whether as a result of Korsakoff's syndrome, Alzheimer's disease, or traumatic injury, is well described as follows: "In amnesics, the process by which distinctive aspects of a situation are selectively attended and selectively reconstituted from their elements

---

[15] Mandler (1980).

[16] Warrington & Weiskrantz (1982).

[17] Wickelgren (1979).

[18] Cohen & Squire (1980).

[19] Jacoby (1983).

[20] For example, Cohen and Squire (1980), Tulving, Schacter, and Stark (1982).

(cues) is compromised. Automatic modes of processing continue unscathed."[21]

The ease with which people recover material when asked to give as responses things that come to mind suggests that psychologists might profitably devote more time to study these everyday occurrences. Much of human memory in everyday situations does not involve the classical retrieval experiments of the psychological laboratory. We tell stories that run on without deliberate search, we interrupt our own and other people's stream of thought with ideas that suddenly "come to mind," we are frequently "reminded" of one or another occurrence in the past, and often we are aware of memories whose apparent irrelevance to the requirements of the moment surprises us. In recent psychological speculations, some thought has been given to the general problem of "reminding," but little systematic work has been undertaken. When it has, it has been directed either at special skills[22] or it has been taxonomic, describing the range of possible nondeliberate thought sequences.[23] However, there may be some benefit to resurrecting an older tradition of the word association studies that were concerned with the automatic access to mental contents.

It seems fruitless to try to unpack the common language sense of "reminding" which subsumes a wide range of disparate phenomena, e.g., "Remind me to go shopping," "That tune reminds me of college," "He reminded me of an old friend," "Tying a knot in a handkerchief is a useful reminder to do something," etc. Instead of trying to explicate the common language, it seems more useful to use a theoretical analysis such as the one presented here, i.e., to make a distinction between automatic and conscious retrievals. Different kinds of memorial situations can then be classified with respect to the mechanisms involved. Further understanding of the automatic effects may give use insights into other kinds of unexplored phenomena. For example, apparently intuitive, irrational memories may often be subsets of automatic recoveries, where events "come to mind" without any deliberate effort and without conscious awareness of the retrieval path.

---

[21] Kinsbourne and Wood (1982, p.214).

[22] For example, Ross (1984).

[23] For example, Shanon (1983).

These automatic "remindings" seem to play a part in all our memorial activities. The discussion of the activation function of conscious contents in Chapter 3 suggests that whenever we are engaged in conscious or deliberate retrieval efforts appropriate segments of the preconscious contents are activated and become more accessible for conscious constructions. Apparently sudden and unintended retrievals during memory searches mark the appearance of conscious waystations that require further processing. This argument also speaks against any single, simple principles of memory retrieval. For example, Endel Tulving has proposed the encoding specificity principle as governing the retrieval of memory traces or records.[24] Originally, the principle made the strong assertion that "cues facilitate recall if and only if the information about [the cues] and about their relation to the to-be-remembered words is stored 'at the same time' as the information about the . . . to-be-remembered words . . . ." This strong version of the encoding specificity principle seems to violate both anecdotal and experimental evidence.[25] Remindings, as just described, seem to lead us very often to information that not only is demanded by the often haphazard cues that are present at any one time, but that clearly was not encoded with them. For example, I see the name "Ironsmith" in a list of references and wonder where I have encountered that name before. It seems familiar until I am reminded of (i.e., there suddenly comes to mind) "Coopersmith," the name of someone whom I do know. The fact that both names share the "...smith" part is not relevant, because it goes counter to the experimental evidence that parts of compound words are ineffective in retrieving the whole, evidence that was originally marshalled for the strong principle.[26] In contrast to the strong version, the modified (weak) version of the encoding specifity principle claims only that "[R]ecollection of an event . . . occurs if and only if properties of the trace of the event are sufficiently similar to the properties of the retrieval information."[27] This modified version is consistent with a wide variety of experimental evidence and most theoretical speculation. The modified principle asserts that some relationship (of unspecified "similarity") must exist between current mental contents and the information that is retrieved. No psychologist would, or could, argue against such an assertion.

---

[24] See Tulving (1983), and also Norman and Bobrow (1979).

[25] See, for example, Anderson and Pichert (1978).

[26] Tulving and Thomson (1973).

[27] Tulving (1983, p. 223).

It is useful to recall again the discussion in Chapter 3 on the construction of conscious contents, specifically in reference to the waystations that become conscious in the process of problem solving or task completion. Consider a master carpenter with much experience in building simple objects such as a kitchen table, who undertakes to work on a special project such as a complex breakfront. In making the table, many of the activities are automatic, and there will be few waystations where choice points occur and conscious processing is invoked. The carpenter will be more or less continuously conscious of the general "building-a-table" schema, and, given the very general nature of this consciousness, other constructions may emerge, such as thinking about last night's ballgame. Under those circumstances, the guiding function of the general schema may be lost; and, if too much interfering mentation takes place, an error or accident may occur. In the case of the more complex breakfront project, the carpenter will have engaged in prior planning, and a variety of schemas and subschemas will have been laid out to guide the carpentry process. Many waystations will occur in the process as particular steps in the building process activate some of the previously established subschemas or steps. These are "remindings" as the carpenter needs to know what he planned to do with a particular door jamb or decorated leg. The carpenter will insist that he needs to concentrate much harder in the process, that his extraneous mentations (such as the ballgame) must be rigorously excluded. He implicitly requires that conscious processes should be concerned only with the task at hand.

Recalling and Recognizing

How about deliberate recall? This is the principal phenomenon of memory performance investigated by psychologists during the last two decades. Experimental subjects are presented with some material, either with or without instructions that they will need to recall it later, and at some subsequent time they are asked for a, usually verbatim, account of the material. As I suggested earlier, this is not the typical, everyday way we use our "memory." Most of the time we are either reminded of something, recognize it, or engage in some combination of the two. We do of course produce deliberate recalls when we try to remember a telephone number, a shopping list, the reference to an interesting experiment we vaguely remember, etc. Frequently, we cannot remember the target material; we have forgotten it. But we also use the term "forgetting" in cases where simple reminding has failed, as, for example, when we forget to stop at the food store on the way home or forget a loved one's birthday. In those cases, we depended on something to activate the relevant mental content so that we would engage in the appropriate activity. But how does deliberate recall proceed?

If any single concept characterizes the cognitive upheaval within the psychology of memory it must be that of organization. Whereas notions of mental organization of experienced or stored material certainly did not arise with the modern cognitive movement,[28] it was the realization that the organization of mental contents made retrieval and recall possible that marked a major change in the tactics and contents of research on memory.[29] It was primarily the appeal to labelled connections that went beyond the prevalent associationism of the late 1950s and early 1960s and contributed to the structural aspect of the cognitive revival. The retrieval of to-be-remembered material was ascribed to the successful use of some organizational structure, and the inability to retrieve the target was thought to be due to the failure of the appropriate organization to be invoked. Organization and structure speak directly to the modified encoding specificity principle. It is exactly the relations among mental contents (their "similarities") that make retrieval possible. If those relations are not invoked by the "cues," then the retrieval attempt will be unsuccessful.

The organizational structures used in memorial retrieval can be grouped into three general prototypes:[30]

1. *Subordinate structures,* in which the organization is hierarchical and particular events are located as subordinate or superordinate to other parts of the structure. These hierarchical structures were of particular interest in the 1960s and the "early" days of uncovering the structure of mental representations. These structures are typically represented in the organization of common categories, but are also assigned to the structure of plans and goals.

2. *Coordinate structures,* in which the organization represents usually mutual and/or symmetric relations among the relevant events. Visual images are a classical example of such structures, where the relations among all the constituent elements define the organization. Unitary, holistic representations, where each constituent is a necessary part of the structure, are coordinate in their use and effect. No part of the structure is in itself sufficient as a mental representation, and all parts are necessary for a complete representation.

---

[28] See, for example, Katona (1940) and Garner (1962).

[29] See Bower (1970), Cofer and Musgrave (1963), Mandler (1967a).

[30] Mandler (1979c).

3. *Proordinate structures* are serially organized. Retrieval of any element of the organization requires the retrieval of a temporally or spatially prior or subsequent event. Most syntactic structures and lists contain substructures of this type.[31]

Having listed these three prototypes, we must note that pure instances of any of them are seldom found. Rather, our memories are typically organized along more than one of these structures. Consider the classical shopping list, which has both serial (proordinate) and categorical (subordinate) components. We list our needs by types (e.g., meat, dairy, cake), and within types may follow the serial structure of a recipe (e.g., for a cake) to list specific ingredients that are wanted. Mnemonic devices, such as the method of loci, or mnemonic rhymes often incorporate all three of these structures. And stories, scripts, and scenes frequently are intricate combinations of all three.[32] Even structures that seem obviously serial, such as the alphabet, are represented in both hierarchical (chunked) and serial structures.[33]

Whatever structure is used in the process of registering events or objects for later construction and use, the notion of relatedness is central to the contemporary treatment of memory. The aforementioned types of structures all have in common the function of principled relations among mental contents. These relations are not neutral links among events (as is fundamental to associationism) but rather define the kind of relationship that is employed--they are labelled.

Clearly, the existence of relations among mental contents illustrates the concept of elaboration discussed in Chapter 2. The more such relations exist between a target schema and other mental contents, the greater the elaboration of the schema and the easier it will be to access, that is, there will be a larger number of possible access routes. The insight that degree of access to memorial contents is a function of the number of possible access routes is not a new one; it goes back to the nonsense syllable era.[34] It was made explicit for the current era initially by the levels of processing concept proposed by Fergus Craik and

---

[31] Traditional verbal learning research approached this tripartite classification in its concern with organized recall, paired-associate learning, and serial acquisitions.

[32] See J. M. Mandler (1984b).

[33] For a theory of serial organization that incorporates both kinds of structures, see Restle (1970).

[34] See, for example, Mandler and Huttenlocher (1956) .

Robert Lockhart.[35] At first, their proposal was that the more deeply (semantically) the target material was initially encoded, the greater was the ease of memorial access. Eventually, this idea was replaced by that of elaboration of processing.[36] If elaboration of a structure or schema contributes to its retrievability, what is the function of the other product of activation discussed in Chapter 2 - the process of integration?

Integration refers to the relations and the mutual activation among the constituents (features) of a schema. The more integrated a structure is, the more easily it is retrieved as a unit, the more distinct it is from other (similar) schemas, and the more likely it is that parts of the schema will activate the whole. Among the consequences of increased activation/integration of a schema are its perceptual fluency[37] and its sense of familiarity. Objects that frequently have been encountered, and are therefore highly integrated, produce the phenomenal sense of familiarity and are more distinctly perceived, in and out of their appropriate context. It should be noted that "familiarity," as I use it, does not refer merely to the ability to identify an object or event as "familiar." Even in the absence of such an identification, actions with respect to objects and events may index the underlying sense of familiarity. Such actions include the ability to move without deliberation in "familiar" environments and judgments about which of two objects has been encountered before or has been encountered more frequently. In other words, "familiarity" is used as a theoretical concept which has, as one of its consequences, the phenomenal experience of familiarity.

The concept of familiarity is central to a discussion of recognition memories. First we must distinguish between two kinds of recognition: One involves only familiarity. It is the sense in which we "recognize" objects that we have encountered before, without necessarily being able to place the last (or first) time when we did so. So-called lexical decision tests, in which letter strings are identified as words or nonwords, build on this kind of knowledge. Familiarity also enters into our knowing our neighborhood or our ability to "recognize" familiar faces or objects (without knowing exactly who the person is or where we have encountered the object before). The other kind of recognition is the one most frequently studied by psychologists, that is, episodic recognition-- placing an event or object in a particular spatiotemporal context. In a typical experiment some objects or events are presented, and the experimental subjects at some later time (varying from minutes to weeks) to discriminate between objects that had been presented and those that

---

[35] Craik and Lockhart (1972).

[36] Craik and Tulving (1975).

[37] Jacoby and Dallas (1981) .

had not. Some 15 years, ago this particular task was identified as requiring a dual-process approach--combining judgments of familiarity with memorial retrieval.[38]

The recognition of previously encountered objects and events is best assigned to the additive and independent probabilities of the event's achieving some criterial familiarity and of the event's being retrievable.[39] The dissociation between the two processes is illustrated in the well-known experience of meeting a person who looks familiar but whose "identity" we are unable to determine at first. The experience usually results in concentrated efforts to retrieve where or when we might have met the person. When we are successful, total recognition has been achieved. The same kind of dissociation can be seen in the performance of anterograde amnesic patients who are unable to recall an event but can, under the right circumstances, perform somewhat better than chance on a recognition test. Their ability to "retrieve" is impaired, but they still are able to perform at a low level of adequacy by using the integrative processes that are not impaired in amnesia.[40]

Short- and Long-Term Memories.

There is one distinction among "memories" that has some claim to empirical and theoretical utility, that is, the division among sensory, short-term, and long-term memory. Sensory (iconic or echoic) memory refers to the information held in a particular sensory modality for a very brief period after stimulation (usually 1 to 2 seconds). The information that is available may subsequently be processed, but the amount of information is highly restricted and the time of its availability is very short.[41]

---

[38] Juola, Fischler, Wood, and Atkinson (1971), Mandler, Pearlstone, and Koopmans (1969).

[39] Mandler (1980, 1981a).

[40] See the discussion above of "reminding" in amnesia.

[41] See Sperling (1960) and Sakitt (1976).

Long-term memory is a rather clumsy term for the information that is stored or retained in an encoded form; it is sometimes coextensive with what has been called (by some) semantic memory and represents the sum total of information and knowledge that an individual has accumulated over a lifetime.

As for short-term memory, there is a need to clear up currently shifting distinctions among such concepts as short-term memory, primary memory, working memory, and consciousness. Short-term memory and primary memory have been used interchangeably,[42] although William James introduced the concept of primary memory as essentially equivalent with the momentary contents of consciousness. Similarly, working memory is frequently referred to as a blackboard conception, coupled with limited capacity. On the other hand, some writers[43] equate short-term memory with momentary consciousness. I prefer to use consciousness to refer to material that is phenomenally immediately available and needs no retrieval and to restrict short-term memory to the limited amount of information that is quickly retrieved, often without the expenditure of processing resources.

The current confusion among different concepts of short term memory may also be resolvable by reference to the activation notion. For example, Klapp, Marshburn, and Lester have drawn attention to the unanalyzed short-term storage concept and its various versions, and they have also shown that the capacity required for a digit span test and that required for more complex information processing are not coextensive.[44] A reasonable solution to this problem is to make a sharp distinction between the current contents of consciousness and material recently encountered but not currently in consciousness. This distinction permits one to distinguish between primary memory, as introduced by William James and which requires no retrieval because it is in fact currently available (in consciousness), and other material that has been recently encountered but requires some additional step to be brought into consciousness. Mental contents that have recently been activated may exhibit a variety of different forms and structures, and different kinds of constructions and processes may be needed to bring them into consciousness. This variety of potentially available material may well be the reason why different short term retrievals have been accorded the status of different memory "systems."

---

42 See, for example, Waugh and Norman (1965).

43 For example, Ericsson and Simon (1980).

44 Klapp, Marshburn, and Lester (1983).

The apparent limitation of short-term memories is not a function of some storage system but rather is the limitation of conscious capacity discussed in the previous chapter. If such capacity is limited (e.g., to 5 or 6 distinct and organized mental events), then anything that is actually retrieved and brought into the conscious state will also display this limitation. Prior activations will make some material more likely to be used for conscious constructions, and it is easy to understand the apparent ease with which material that was encountered some seconds earlier may be retrieved. However, we are equally able to bring into consciousness material activated during the preceding hours, the state-of-the-world memory that I discuss presently.

This view of different short-term memories distinguishes also between limited conscious capacity and the working memory locution. The working memory idea has been most convincingly developed by Baddeley and his associates.[45] They have proposed a central executive function assisted by various modality controlled loops and memory systems (e.g., articulatory and visuospatial). These ancillary systems can best be seen as providing input to the memory function, if that is conceived as the conscious construction that is the final stage of a memorial process. In that view, a number of different ancillary processes may provide input to the final product, including rehearsal processes, place-holding functions, acoustic codes etc. New processes, such as information-storing motor skills, may be acquired or adopted and thus can extend working memory which has no capacity limits as such.[46]

Episodic and Semantic Memories

A distinction between two kinds of memories that has received a renewed following during recent years is that between episodic and semantic memories introduced by Tulving.[47] At a general level, episodic memories involve "the recording and subsequent retrieval of memories of personal happenings and doings," whereas semantic memories deal with "knowledge of the world that is independent of a person's identity

---

[45] Baddeley (1976), Baddeley and Hitch (1974).

[46] Reisberg, Rappaport, and O'Shaughnessy (1984).

[47] See Tulving (1983) for an extensive presentation, including the history of the distinction.

and past."[48] The distinction has great heuristic value and is phenomenally immediately appealing. It presents a ready and comprehensible way of dividing up different kinds of experiments as well as subjective experiences. On the other hand, it is questionable whether these two kinds of memories represent different systems, with different rules or laws governing their operation. At the simplest level, it is obvious that episodic memories draw on semantic knowledge (a point that is not disputed). But semantic memories also have "personal" characteristics. It is unlikely that different people's knowledge of foods, or bears, or history is unaffected by the personal conditions under which it is acquired. Nor can it be argued for long that episodic memories are any less conceptually organized than semantic ones, or that they are primarily (or even uniquely) temporally organized. For example, our (semantic) knowledge of historical events is often mainly temporally organized, whereas my memory of how I played a game of chess or the pictures I saw at an exhibition may well be conceptually organized by opening gambits or genre.

One of the distinctions that has been claimed for the episodic semantic differentiation is that anterograde amnesic patients suffer from a defect in episodic but not semantic memory.[49] However, as I noted before, that dissociation falls rather nicely under the rubric of activation *per se* vs. conscious access, and no new memory systems are needed to understand the phenomenon. In addition, memory loss in amnesic patients seems to cut across the episodic/semantic distinction; intact performance cannot be assigned merely to semantic information but rather to any information that was acquired before the onset of the amnesia, whether semantic or episodic.[50] Other evidence that the distinction at best describes conditions of acquisition shows that priming effects cannot be differentiated on episodic and semantic grounds.[51] The distinction is "a potentially useful way of classifying different types of knowledge and not as a description of two separate memory systems."[52]

---

[48] Tulving (1983, p. 9).

[49] See, for example, Horton and Mills (1984).

[50] Baddeley and Wilson (1983) .

[51] McKoon and Ratcliffe (1979); see also Dosher (1984).

[52] McCloskey and Santee (1981, p.71).

LEARNING

Until the 1950s, learning and motivation were the reigning king and queen of American psychology. It is sometimes difficult to comprehend their demise in the ensuing 30 years, but cognitive psychologists were either preoccupied with the steady state organism or unsure how to handle the problem of cognitive change until they understood what it is that changes during learning. Usually they were willing to leave the problem to their friendly neighbors in cognitive development, and it has been the latter who have occupied center stage in considerations of learning and acquisition. The highly sophisticated, creative, and productive work in language acquisition is the prime example of the study of "learning" in cognitive psychology.[53] However, cognitive development has been seen as the vehicle for studying learning in other areas, such as number use,[54] as well. In most areas, though probably less so in language development, the major instigation has been Piaget's theory.[55]

When we look at cognitive psychologists' attempts to deal with problems of learning, we find little new beyond rediscoveries of Piaget and his concepts. The most widely accepted concepts about the change of schemas are Piaget's concepts of accommodation and assimilation.[56] *Accommodation* refers to the case in which a new experience is such that existing structures (schemas) cannot accept the new information; structures must be changed in order to take account of it. As a result, our view of the world is changed as it includes the novel experience as a legitimate part of a new perceptual or conceptual structure or adapts existing action structures to accommodate the new demands and information. A prototypical case of accommodation can be found in the young child as accumulating experiences build up a model of his or her world. Even for the adult, however, accommodation takes place when we learn something new. For example, when we learn to drive a car with a clutch (having previously used only automatic transmission), our schema for driving is changed, and when we switch from a dial to a push-button telephone, our telephone schema changes. In the case of *assimilation,* on the other hand, existing structures remain unchanged,

---

[53] See, for example, Gleitman and Wanner (1982), Felix and Wode (1982).

[54] Gelman and Gallistel (1978).

[55] See J.M. Mandler (1983).

[56] Piaget (1970).

but the interpretation of the world is changed in order to deal adequately with a slightly changed situation, for example, meeting somebody at a party and finding the initial conversation about a painting puzzling because the other person talks about shadings while we see brilliant color. We might accommodate these new opinions to a new structure, but we simply assimilate when we discover that the other person is colorblind. No change in our existing mental organization is needed. Most cases of categorization and stereotyping are cases of assimilation.

Accommodation and assimilation are obviously extremes of a continuum of potential change in mental structures. But what about the case in which an event (conceptual, perceptual, or action demanding) cannot be handled by accommodation or assimilation? Events that cannot be assimilated or accommodated present a special problem for mental theory. In principle, they should not be registered. Some psychologists have argued that events that do not fit any current schemas cannot be perceived at all. Thus, opening a kitchen cupboard and being presented with a snarling lion would be a non-event. Such a conclusion would be both foolish and theoretically sterile. The mental system handles such situations in a variety of ways, first by searching for hypotheses and schemas that *can* handle the new evidence. These immediate attempts at accommodation often produce relatively unstructured results, as in the identification of a vague shadow, an unfamiliar noise, or an unidentifiable taste or smell. In fact, as we see later, the cognitive processing of interruptions and discrepancies plays a major role in the construction of emotion.

Schemas change, spin off new ones, are incorporated into others, and develop superordinate relations to each other. Such hierarchical relations and organization seem to be a natural choice for the larger organization of schematic structures. These organizations support our general proclivity to see things not only as "part of" others but also as examples of more general or abstract notions. Shinbones are not only connected to kneebones, which are connected to thighbones, all to the greater glory of the whole human body, but toes are parts of feet, are parts of legs, are parts of human bodies, are parts of animal organisms, are parts of living things. Similarly, apples are fruits, are plants, are organic things.

Structures are not as neatly ordered as a simple hierarchy may indicate; a better expression is found in the idea of a heterarchy, where superordinate and subordinate relations exist but where these relations may shift from requirement to requirement and where, within a particular concept, there may be assembled a number of equivalent, unordered features, attributes, or schemas. As an example of the development of schemas, consider a child learning about dogs. The schema about "dogs" will develop out of the early instances and the early discriminations. Assume that the first experience a child has is with a large, black dog that barks frequently. The unspoken, prelinguistic meaning[57] of this concept thus involves something moving, something black, and also something that, because of sudden barking noises, may have attached to it a degree of autonomic arousal. This initial experience is elaborated on subsequent occasions. However, the initial "dog" schema may have connections to a structure, presumably present before the first experience with a dog, that makes distinctions between stationary and moving objects. As experience with dogs increases, the schema of dog is discriminated into both generic and embedded schemas of small ones, nonblack ones, ones that do not bark, and also ones that lick your hand, that fetch things, and so forth. At the same time, there are characteristics of dogs (e.g., they are self propelled objects) that will produce generalizations and coordination with high-level schemas, including those relating to living things, or, for example, the common schema that includes cats and dogs, which refers to them as tame domestic animals usually found in the home. We thus assume that "lower" or "higher" schemas develop from initial schemas in a hierarchical system. But, if the initial instance is extensively processed, then despite the development of the schema and its generalization and discrimination, reference will frequently return to that initial schema. If the child's attention has been particularly drawn to the initial large, black, barking dog, then that may well, to a very large extent, characterize its schema of dogs and even the general meaning of pets.

The interaction among generic and instantiated schemas also illustrates the development and growth of schemas. Any specific experience with a particular event not only establishes a sometimes transitory schema of its own but also contributes to the expected values of the variables of a more generic schema. Consider the story of the father and son who were involved in an accident. The father dies, and the son is brought to the hospital emergency unit, where the surgeon exclaims: "My God, that's my son". The story is surprising because our traditional surgeon schemas identify surgeons as being male. Changing that value of the surgeon variable to being gender neutral is a long pro-

---

[57] Macnamara (1972).

cess, brought about in part by hearing a story like this one.

There is a hangover from earlier days that still characterizes many psychological speculations about learning. It is the idea that learning is unitary function/process of the organism (and even of all organisms). The schematic locution leaves open the question *how* some of the changes come about. It is fairly obvious that learning a maze (whether in a laboratory or in downtown Boston) requires feedback, acquisitions of cognitive maps, and other mechanisms. The acquisition of an object concept--how to differentiate flowers from their surrounds, for example--involves no feedback but much in the way of incorporating consistency and feature correlations, as well as higher order concepts such as object constancy. Learning to like certain foods again involves sheer presentation in many cases but may have little to do with rein-forcement, feedback, or any of the constancies. In short, learning can come about in a a number of ways, some of which we may not even have begun to explore.

Parenthetically, the pluralistic view of learning should also encourage a similar attitude towards theories of human inferential thinking and problems solving. In contrast to those who take a unitary view that suggests that a single, fundamental set of mechanisms supports all such "thinking,"[58] the evidence suggests that the complexity and pliability of the human mind (and brain) can spawn a variety of different ways of solving problems and arrive at complex conclusions. Among these are important and complex ones such as the mental models approach advo-cated by Johnson-Laird. But they also include propositional logic, sim-ple (almost reflexive) beliefs, activation driven remindings, and many other ways of structuring the world and solving its problems.

The Challenge of Conditioning

Cognitive psychologists, particularly of more recent generations, tend to be both ignorant and disdainful of the animal learning and condition-ing literature. The disdain may in part be justified because of the failure of the conditioning paradigms significantly to illuminate human functioning; the ignorance creates other difficulties. It is not unusual for psychologists (cognitive and otherwise) to ascribe to "conditioning" some phenomenon that they fail to understand. What is usually meant is that there must have been some concatenation of events in the past that has brought about the current state of affairs. In fact, of course, the conditioning literature is full of reliable observations that cry for

---

[58] For example, J.R. Anderson (1982) and Johnson-Laird (1983).

theoretical explication. To ascribe something to conditioning explains very little, and it does not avoid having to provide some theoretical account. And there are enough phenomena that have been ascribed to conditioning (such as the "conditioning" of autonomic nervous system responses, of some meanings, of beliefs, etc.) to evoke serious concern with both the data and the necessary theory.

For example, one could approach the conditioning paradigm in terms of schema theory. It has by now been generally accepted that in order to be effective the conditioned stimulus must provide some degree of predictability, i.e., conditioning depends on the contingency between the conditioned and unconditioned stimulus.[59] In other words, the conditioned stimulus, like the schema, has the function of providing reliable expectations of environmental contingencies. Different kinds of conditioning paradigms require different kinds of analyses. In the case of aversive conditioning, in which a tone and a shock might be paired, it is highly likely that the response to the conditioned stimulus (the tone) is not just an unconditioned response that has been shifted to the conditioned stimulus.[60] The situations are different; the organism responds to them differently and needs different representations for them. In the case of the unconditioned response to the shock, it must deal with a specific noxious event. However, when the conditioned stimulus alone is presented, the organism is faced with the problem of not having available an action (such as escape) that could cope with an impending (signaled) aversive event. In the case of eyelid conditioning, the unconditioned stimulus is a puff of air and the unconditioned response is an eye blink. The latter is obviously a well-established (probably innate) defensive response. The schema of tone-air puff is one in which the tone signals a noxious, negatively evaluated event that is escapable, and the action schema of tone-eyeblink-air puff is established. Here the tone is the signal not for an unsolvable but for a solvable problem. In the case of salivary conditioning, meat powder produces salivation, as does a tone paired with the meat powder. Here again, the anticipation is different. The meat powder stimulates salivation. The schema of tone-meatpowder-salivation embodies the expectation of (organized) eating activity and eventually elicits preparatory salivation.

---

[59] Rescorla (1967).

[60] See, for example, Obrist, Sutterer, and Howard (1972).

Obviously, I have not done justice to the conditioning literature; rather, I have tried to highlight some obvious areas that deserve more cognitive attention. My purpose is to show the generality of a cognitive approach that seeks to understand the underlying representations for observable organismic actions.[61] Much of the information made available by the conditioning paradigm remains to be mined by cognitive psychologists. For example, the available information about the effect of varying CS-US intervals should provide much needed information about the temporal organization of schemas.

EMOTION

Edwin Guthrie is reported to have remarked that Edward Tolman's paleo-cognitive theory leaves the animal at a choice point lost in thought. If Tolman's animals were unable to act, much of contemporary cognitive theory seems to leave human beings unable to feel. Until recently, conventional wisdom in cognitive science painted people without passions, thinking and acting rationally and cooly. If cognitive science is supposed to encompass all of psychology,[62] then at least cognitive psychology should do so. And if cognitive psychology aspires to an understanding of human thought and action, it can ill afford to leave out their emotional aspects.

Emotion is not only anecdotally and phenomenally part of human thought and action, there is now a burgeoning body of evidence that emotional states interact in important ways with traditional "cognitive" functions. For example, positive feelings determine the accessibility of mental contents in the process of decision making, serve as retrieval cues, and influence problem-solving strategies.[63] More generally, accessibility of mental contents is determined by the mood both at the time of original encounter and at the time of retrieval.[64] Thus, emotion should be of both general and specific interest to cognitive psychologists. I explore a cognitive view of emotional experience that I have

---

[61] See also Gallistel (1980).

[62] Norman (1980).

[63] Isen and Means (1983), Isen, Means, Patrick, and Nowicki (1982), Isen, Shalker, Clark, and Karp (1978).

[64] Bower (1981).

developed at length elsewhere.[65] I start with a view of different approaches to emotion in order to motivate a cognitive constructivist approach.

The Construction of Emotion

There are essentially two different views of emotional phenomena. One considers emotions to be discrete patterns of behavior, experience, and neural activity, usually consisting of some few (5 to 10) such patterns--the fundamental emotions, such as fear, joy, and rage.[66] These are seen as having developed as a function of human (and mammalian) evolution, with other emotions being combinations of the fundamental ones. Given the wide variety of human emotion, this latter postulate engenders complex analyses of and recipes for emotion, something like a cordon bleu school of emotion. The other approach is cognitive and constructivist, considering emotional experience (and behavior) to be the result of cognitive analyses and physiological (autonomic nervous system) response.[67] The constructivist approach has as its founding father William James, though his particular constructions are no longer found acceptable. The father of the fundamentalist approach is, of course, Charles Darwin.

There exists another argument in the field of emotion concerning the character of emotional (or affective) reactions. This argument is related to, but somewhat different from, the fundamental/constructive division. The distinction here is between a constructivist view of emotional reactions (specifically subjective feelings) and one that distinguishes between affective (emotional) and "cognitive" analyses. The foremost practitioner of the latter approach is Robert Zajonc.[68] He has marshalled an impressive array of anecdotal and phenomenal evidence to argue that affective responses are unmediated and fast initial reactions to people and events. Affective reactions respond (without mediating "cognitive" analyses) to specific aspects of the event, to the extent of stipulating specific characteristics of events that force preferences (so-called preferanda). The response of a cognitive constructivist is the same as it

---

[65] Mandler (1984b).

[66] See, for example, Izard (1971) and Tomkins (1981).

[67] See, for example, Averill (1980), Lazarus, Kanner, and Folkman (1980), Mandler (1984b).

[68] Zajonc (1980, 1984).

is to the ecological Gibsonian approach to perception. Whatever the array of attributes and features in the environment might be, it needs analysis and processing by underlying representations. Specifically, the phenomenal evidence of initially affective reactions to events is not, by itself, evidence for an unmediated affective response.[69] Affective experiences are constructed conscious contents, just like any other such content. The indisputable observation that we frequently react affectively to events, before experiencing a more "analytic" knowledge of the event, speaks to the primacy of affective and evaluational constructions and intentions. We live in a world of value and affect, and the themes that often determine our conscious constructions require an affective content. This does not force an absence of other analyses and activations going on at the same time at the preconscious level. Which of these analyses will be used in conscious constructions will depend on the intentions and requirements of the moment, which happen to be "affective" in many cases. On the other hand, the assertion of "fast" affective reactions is an empirical one. If, in fact, affective, evaluative reactions are faster than those requiring only access to cognitions (knowledge), then one would have to reconsider the constructivist argument. However, the available evidence suggests that affective reactions are actually *slower* than "cognitive" ones.[70] Such a finding is consistent with the notion that questions about the familiarity or identity of objects or events require access to relatively fewer features of the underlying representation and can be quickly constructed, in comparison with more extensive analyses and constructions required by questions about the appeal, beauty, or desirability of the object or event.

The construction of emotion in general (at least as seen by this practitioner) consists of the concatenation in consciousness of some cognitive evaluative schema together with the perception of visceral arousal. This conscious construction is, like all others, a holistic unitary experience, even though it may derive from separate and even independent schematic representations (see Chapter 3). This attitude toward emotion depends on an approximation of the commonsense meaning of the term. The question "What is an emotion?" is not, in principle, answerable. The term is a natural language expression that has all the advantages (communicative and inclusive) and disadvantages (imprecise and vague) of the common language that were discussed in Chapter 1. However, it is exactly for communicative purposes that one needs to approximate the common meaning as a first step. Among the possible analyses of common language "emotions," I have focused on two

---

69 It is, in fact, a demonstration of the phenomenocentrism I discussed earlier.

70 Mandler and Shebo (1983).

characteristics: the idea that emotions express some aspect of value, and the assertion that emotions are "hot"--they imply a gut reaction, a visceral response. These two aspects not only speak to the common usage, but also reflect a frequent conscious construction. Thus, an analysis of the concatenation of value and visceral arousal addresses both natural language usage and a theoretically important problem. One of the consequences of such a position is that it leads to the postulation of innumerable emotional states, no situational evaluation being the same from occasion to occasion. There are of course regularities in human thought and action that produce general categories of these constructions, categories that have family resemblances and overlap in the features that are selected for analysis and that create the representation of value (whether it is the simple dichotomy of good and bad, or the appreciation of beauty, or the perception of evil). These families of occasions and meanings construct the categories of emotions found in the natural language (and psychology). The commonalities found within these categories may vary from case to case. Sometimes they are based on the similarity of external conditions (as in the case of some fears and environmental threats), sometimes they share similar behaviors (in the subjective feelings of fear related to flight), sometimes they arise from incipient behavior (as in hostility and destructive action), sometimes from hormonal and physiological reactions (as in the case of lust), and sometimes from purely cognitive evaluations (as judgments of helplessness eventuate in anxiety). It is these commonalities that give rise to the appearance of fundamental or discrete emotions. However, these conglomerations are not haphazard collections; they are organized by their conditions and states, whether their source is behavioral, cognitive, or physiological. The source for their discreteness can be found in those conditions, rather than in a fundamental (biological) identity of their subjective feeling states. And even these "fundamental" emotional states require some analytic, "cognitive" processing. Emotions are frequently situation specific, and subjective emotional states, however one defines their source, need to be tied to some cognitive evaluations that "select" the appropriate emotion.

The problem of *cognitive evaluation* seems therefore common to all emotion theories. In recent years there has been much active search for the basis of these valuative structures.[71] Basically, cognitive evaluations require a theory for the representation of value. What is the mental representation that gives rise to judgments and feelings of "good" or "bad" or of some affective nature in general? I suggest three such sources:

---

[71] See, for example, Bower and Cohen (1982), Ortony, Collins, and Clore (1982).

1. Innate approach and withdrawal tendencies interpreted as value. The avoidance of looming objects, the experience of pain (and the avoidance of pain-producing objects), and the taste of sweet substances are all examples of events that produce approach and avoidance reactions. It is the secondary effects of these tendencies, such as our observations of our own approaches and withdrawals, that produce the judgments of positive and negative values.

2. Cultural, social, and idiosyncratic predication, which is the process by which objects, whether actually encountered or not, are predicated to have certain values as a result of social or personal learning experiences. Food preferences and aversions (such as frogs' legs and chocolate cake) are frequently acquired without any contact with the actual substances, as are likes and dislikes of people and groups of people. These predications, socially and idiosyncratically acquired, produce judgments of value. Similarly constituted are the culturally acquired esthetic judgments of beauty, whether of people, landscapes, or paintings.

3. Structural value, which resides in the cognitive structure of objects, in the relations among features, as in the appreciation of an object seen as beautiful or abhorrent as a function of a particular structural concatenation. Structural value, which differentiates patterns rather than mere identification of objects, arises out of our experience with objects and the analyses of their constituent features. One of the factors that influence judgments arising out of structural consideration is the frequency of encounter with objects and events, as, for example, in the experience of familiarity.

The problem of value in general, whether in connection with emotion or as an interesting representational question for its own sake, has long been avoided by psychologists, of whatever theoretical stripe. However, it is not an issue that can long be avoided if we are truly interested in the full range of human thought and action.

If evaluative cognitions provide the quality of an emotional experience, then visceral activity provides its intensity and peculiar "emotional" feel. It can be argued that visceral arousal usually follows the occurrence of some perceptual or cognitive discrepancy or the interruption or blocking of some ongoing action. Such discrepancies and interruptions depend to a large extent on the organization of mental representation of thought and action. Within the purview of schema theory, these discrepancies occur when the expectations of some schema (whether determining thought or action) are violated. This is the case whether the violating event is worse or better than the expected one, and these discrepancies account for visceral arousal in both unhappy and joyful occasions. Most emotions follow such discrepancies, just because the discrepancy produces visceral arousal. And it is the combination of that arousal with an ongoing evaluative cognition that produces the subjective experience of an emotion. The effects of situational or life stress are excellent examples of unexpected events producing visceral arousal, negative evaluations, and emotional experiences.[72]

Finally, the construction of emotions requires conscious capacity. The very experience of emotion is, by definition, a conscious state and thus preempts limited capacity. As a result, emotional experiences frequently are not conducive to the full utilization of our cognitive apparatus, and thought may become simplified, i.e., stereotyped and canalized, and will tend to revert to simpler modes of thought and problem solving. However, the effects are not necessarily intrusive and deleterious. It will depend, in part, on other mental contents that are activated by the emotional experience and that may become available for dealing with situations as well as mental events. The relationship of "emotions" to discrepancies and autonomic nervous system recruitment also points to their adaptive function; emotions occur at important times in the life of the organism and may serve to prepare it for more effective thought and action when focused attention is needed.

Emotions provide a prime example of the multi- and overdetermination of human thought and action. We do not live in our world with simple, single expectations, and similarly their violations (the discrepancies) are not unidimensional. Unconscious expectations of the state of the world not only encompass a large number of different aspects of our environment at the same time, but also involve conflicting expectations about the same event. One important example is found in many positive emotional states. The intensity of these states is often related to the fact that at the same time that we expect (hope for) the positive outcome, we also "expect" the negative one. The intense delight of a student at receiving a high grade on an examination is probably in part related to her uncertainty, that is, a mixture of expecting the good grade together with the possibility that she might get a lower grade. It is the latter expectation that is violated and provides additional arousal and as a result, and together with the positive state engendered by the high grade, a positive emotional state is generated. Another student may receive the lower grade and his disappointment will be further potentiated by the vilolation of his positive expectation. Similar concatenations, often involving more than two activated schemas (and expectations) are found everyday in the job situation, in close relationships, and even in rather mundane scenarios such as the dentist's office, a restaurant, or in a food market.

---

[72] See Berscheid (1983) for a related and ingenious analysis of close relationships.

PSYCHOLOGY AND HUMAN EXPERIENCE

With the discussion of emotion I have come full circle to some of the themes of Chapter 1. Cognitive psychology, of all the cognitive sciences, must take responsibility for exploring those aspects of cognition that are uniquely human. Central to these is consciousness. I have argued for such a a point of view both in Chapter 3 and in the special applications in this chapter. However, until now the discussions of conscious constructions have had an all-or-none flavor--either a cognitive structure participates in a conscious state or it does not. However, it has generally been recognized that there are potential and partially realized actions and thoughts that seem to hover on the edge of consciousness. I wish to talk about these in terms of a state-of-the-world knowledge that is primarily dependent on ongoing activations as a result of both our intercourse with the external world and our own mental activities.[73] Although relatively little is known about the course of activation--how schema activation decays and how that decay apparently differs for different kinds of structures--we can safely assume that, once activated, many mental structures maintain an increased level of activation for some reasonable lenght of time.

Our ongoing experience of the world continuously updates the values of variables within cognitive structures, both specific and general. Starting with one's morning activities, and probably with residues from the previous night's dreams, schemas relevant to having breakfast, getting dressed, planning the day's activities, interacting with one's family, all are activated and probably stay in a state of activation for some time to come. As the day proceeds, more and more previously unconscious schemas are activated, though not necessarily used in conscious constructions. The set of activated mental structures defines our state-of-the-world knowledge. Evidence from events in the world, thoughts about today's and previous activities, in short, all we do and think affects the structures and schemas of our unconscious and activates them. These directly or indirectly activated representations may subsequently be easily and often automatically brought into consciousness. Constructions involving currently active schemas come to mind seemingly without effort; they have the phenomenal appearance of hovering close to consciousness. No deliberation is needed to determine who I am, where I am, or what I am doing, even though I may not have been consciously thinking about any of these knowledges just prior to their realization. These preconscious structures determine our immediate

---

[73] I am grateful to Roy D'Andrade for extensive discussions that permitted the development of these notions.

expectations as well as our current state. These expectations (and their underlying schemas) are continuously updated. As I sit in my office, I "know" that I am the only person there, until a colleague comes in and asks to look at some journals. I return to my work, without consciously thinking about her, but I now "know" that there is somebody else there and I will not be surprised to hear her ask a question. These current activations determine the current "meaning" of the world around us; they are representative not only of our immediate experience with the world but also of wider themes. Both worldly and internal interactions activate specific and concrete schemas on the one hand and more general categories and schemas on the other. A particular interaction may have activated a representation of cooperation and helping which will in turn exert its influence on subsequent interactions. Solitary musings about some of yesterday's events or about a long-past experience will also make available those structures for interactions with current events. Finally, as some psychologists seem to forget at times, action and thought, and the activation of the relevant cognitive structures, are both multi- and over-determined. Conscious constructions will be determined by a large variety of current and past experiences that have - for one reason or another - produced relevant activations at the preconscious level.

Emotional experiences are also actually or potentially with us in the same state-of-the-world activations. I indicated previously that interruptions and discrepancies are, if not a necessary, certainly a sufficient condition for visceral arousal and possible subsequent emotions. However, in Chapter 3 I noted that changes in contents of consciousness are, to a large extent, due to failures of expectations, changes in the currently experienced state of the world. If both of these statements are a reasonable reflection of mental life, it follows that some kind of emotional states are likely to be a constant feature of an active mind. These "emotional" states are relatively weak and transient; discrepancies may produce changes in conscious contents but very weak visceral changes. Absent important and drastic changes in our world, these "little emotions" color our ongoing life; they do not usually dominate it.

If modern cognitive psychology is to live up to its promise to the cognitive science enterprise by providing an integrated view of human beings, it will have to be concerned with the issues that I have approached here. It will also have to tackle more esoteric topics, including esthetics, dreams, play, and ethics. Among the experiences and ascriptions of our phenomenal world that need analysis are concepts such as rationality and will. Many of these are embedded in our culture, and we will need to work with anthropologists and sociologists to achieve a better understanding of them. But the task is the same as with other human chracteristics--to show how underlying representations and processes generate these very human products and qualities. In sum, cognitive psychology could have all of human experience as its purview. Such a view of the human condition is more lifelike than a picture of a coldly analytic processor accumulating knowledge and memory. Too often, cognitive science has presented such a robot-like picture of human beings. In contrast, I believe that a theoretically consistent "cognitive" approach to psychology can be responsive to the realities of human social and individual experience.

References

Ackley, D. H., Hinton, G. E., & Sejnowski, T. J. (1985). Learning and communication in Boltzmann machines. *Cognitive Science*, in press.

Adrian, E. D. (1966). Consciousness. In J. C. Eccles (Ed.), *Brain and conscious experience*. New York: Springer.

Anderson, J. R. (1976). *Language, memory, and thought*. Hillsdale, NJ: Lawrence Erlbaum Associates.

Anderson, J. R. (1982). Acquisition of cognitive skill. *Psychological Review*, *89*, 369-406.

Anderson, J. R. (1983). *The architecture of cognition*. Cambridge, MA: Harvard University Press.

Anderson, N. H. (1981). *Foundations of information integration theory*. New York: Academic Press.

Anderson, R. C., & Pichert, J. W. (1978). Recall of previously unrecallable information following a shift in perspective. *Journal of Verbal Learning and Verbal Behavior*, *17*, 1-12.

Anderson, R. E. (1984). Did I do it or did I imagine doing it? *Journal of Experimental Psychology: General*, *113*, 594-613.

Atkinson, R. C., & Shiffrin, R. M. (1968). Human memory: A proposed system and its control processes. In K. W. Spence & J. T. Spence (Eds.), *The psychology of learning and motivation* (Vol. 2). New York: Academic Press.

Averill, J. R. (1980). A constructivist view of emotion. In R. Plutchik & H. Kellerman (Eds.), *Theories of emotion*. New York: Academic Press.

Baars, B. J. (1983). Conscious contents provide the nervous system with coherent global information. In R. J. Davidson, G. E. Schwartz, & D. Shapiro (Eds.), *Consciousness and self-regulation* (Vol. 3). New York: Plenum.

Baddeley, A. D. (1976). *The psychology of memory*. New York: Harper and Row.

Baddeley, A. D., & Hitch, G. (1974). Working memory. In G. H. Bower (Ed.), *The psychology of learning and motivation* (Vol. 8). New York: Academic Press.

Baddeley, A. D., & Wilson, B. (1983). *Amnesia and the distinction between semantic and episodic memory*. Paper presented at the July 1983 meeting of the Experimental Psychology Society, Oxford, England.

Bain, A. (1875). *The emotions and the will* (Third edition). London: Longmans, Green.

Bartlett, F. C. (1932). *Remembering*. Cambridge: Cambridge University Press.

Berscheid, E. (1983). Emotion. In H. H. Kelley, E. Berscheid, A. Christensen, J. H. Harvey, T. L. Hudson, G. Levinger, E. McClintock, L. A. Peplau, & D. R. Peterson, *Close relationships*. San Francisco: Freeman.

Bobrow, D. G., & Winograd, T. (1977). An overview of KRL, a knowledge representation language. *Cognitive Science, 1*, 3-46.

Bousfield, W. A. (1953). The occurrence of clustering in the recall of randomly arranged associates. *Journal of General Psychology, 49*, 229-240.

Bower, G. H. (1970). Organizational factors in memory. *Cognitive Psychology, 1*, 18-46.

Bower, G. H. (1981). Mood and memory. *American Psychologist, 36*, 129-148.

Bower, G. H., & Cohen, P. (1982). Emotional influences in memory and thinking: Data and theory. In M. S. Clark & S. T. Fiske (Eds.), *Affect and cognition: The Seventeenth Annual Carnegie symposium on cognition*. Hillsdale, NJ: Lawrence Erlbaum Associates.

Bowlby, J. (1969). *Attachment* (Attachment and Loss, Vol. 1). London: Hogarth Press and Institute of Psychoanalysis.

Broadbent, D. E. (1958). *Perception and communication*. London: Pergamon Press.

Bruner, J. S., Goodnow, J. J., & Austin, G. A. (1956). *A study of thinking.* New York: Wiley.

Bush, R. R., & Mosteller, F. (1955). *Stochastic models for learning.* New York: Wiley.

Cartwright, N. (1983). *How the laws of physics lie.* New York: Oxford University Press.

Chen, L. (1982). Topological structure in visual perception. *Science, 218*, 699-700.

Chomsky, N. (1956). Three models for the description of language. *IRE Transactions on Information Theory, IT-2(3)*, 113-124.

Chomsky, N. (1957). *Syntactic structures.* The Hague: Mouton.

Clarke, R., & Morton, J. (1983). Cross modality facilitation in tachistoscopic word recognition. *Quarterly Journal of Experimental Psychology, 35A*, 79-96.

Cofer, C. N. (1961). *Verbal learning and verbal behavior.* New York: McGraw-Hill.

Cofer, C. N., & Musgrave, B. S. (1963). *Verbal behavior and learning.* McGraw-Hill.

Cohen, N. J., & Squire, L. R. (1980). Preserved learning and retention of pattern analyzing skill in amnesia: Dissociation of knowing how and knowing that. *Science, 210*, 207-209.

Coltheart, M., Patterson, K. E., & Marshall, J. C. (Eds.) (1980). *Deep dyslexia.* London: Routledge and Kegan Paul.

Craik, F. I. M., & Lockhart, R. S. (1972). Levels of processing: A framework for memory research. *Journal of Verbal Learning and Verbal Behavior, 11*, 671-684.

Craik, F. I. M., & Tulving, E. (1975). Depth of processing and the retention of words in episodic memory. *Journal of Experimental Psychology: General, 104*, 268-294.

Craik, K. J. W. (1943). *The nature of explanation.* Cambridge: Cambridge University Press.

Craik, K. J. W. (1966). *The nature of psychology* (edited by S. L. Sherwood). Cambridge: Cambridge University Press.

Cutting, J. E. (in preparation). *Perception, projection, and optic fields.*

Cutting, J. E., & Millard, R. T. (1984). Three gradients and the perception of flat and curved surfaces. *Journal of Experimental Psychology: General, 113*, 198-216.

Dempster, F. N. (1981). Memory span: Sources of individual and developmental differences. *Psychological Bulletin, 89*, 63-100.

Deutsch, J. A., & Deutsch, D. (1963). Attention: Some theoretical considerations. *Psychological Review, 70*, 80-90.

Donders, F. C. (1862). Die Schnelligkeit psychischer Processe. *Archiv für Anatomie und Physiologie*, 657-681.

Dosher, B. A. (1984). Discriminating preexperimental (semantic) from learned (episodic) associations: A speed-accuracy study. *Cognitive Psychology*, *16*, 519-555.

Ebbinghaus, H. (1885). *Ueber das Gedächtnis: Untersuchungen zur experimentellen Psychologie*. Leipzig: Duncker und Humblot.

Ericsson, K. A., & Simon, H. (1980). Verbal reports as data. *Psychological Review*, *87*, 215-251.

Felix, S. W., & Wode, H. (Eds.) (1982). *Language development at the crossroads*. Tübingen: Gunter Narr Verlag.

Fodor, J. A. (1983). *The modularity of mind*. Cambridge, MA: The MIT Press.

Fowler, C. A., Wolford, G., Slade, R., & Tassinary, L. (1981). Lexical access with and without awareness. *Journal of Experimental Psychology: General*, *110*, 341-362.

Franks, J. J., & Bransford, J. D. (1971). Abstraction of visual patterns. *Journal of Experimental Psychology*, *90*, 65-74.

Freud, S. (1900). The interpretation of dreams. In *The Standard Edition of the Complete Psychological Works of Sigmund Freud* (Vols. 4 and 5). London: Hogarth Press, 1975.

Frijda, N. H., & deGroot, A. D. (Eds.) (1981). *Otto Selz: His contribution to psychology*. The Hague: Mouton.

Gallistel, C. R. (1974). Motivation as central organizing process: The psychophysical approach to its functional and neurophysiological analysis. In J. K. Cole & T. B. Sonderegger (Eds.), *Nebraska symposium on motivation: 1974*. Lincoln, Neb: University of Nebraska Press.

Gallistel, C. R. (1980). *The organization of action: A new synthesis*. Hillsdale, NJ: Lawrence Erlbaum Associates.

Garner, W. R. (1962). *Uncertainty and structure as psychological concepts*. New York: Wiley.

Gelman, R., & Gallistel, C. R. (1978). *The child's understanding of number*. Cambridge: Harvard University Press.

Gentner, D., & Stevens, A. (Eds.) (1982). *Mental models*. Hillsdale, NJ: Lawrence Erlbaum Associates.

Gibson, J. J. (1966). *The senses considered as perceptual systems*. Boston: Houghton Mifflin.

Gleitman, L., & Wanner, E. (Eds.) (1982). *Language acquisition: The state of the art*. Cambridge, MA: Harvard University Press.

Goodenough, W. H. (1956). Componential analysis and the study of meaning. *Language*, *32*, 195-216.

Graesser, A. C., & Mandler, G. (1978). Limited processing capacity constrains the storage of unrelated sets of words and retrieval from natural categories. *Journal of Experimental Psychology: Human Learning and Memory*, *4*, 86-100.

Graf, P., Mandler, G., & Haden, P. (1982). Simulating amnesic symptoms in normal subjects. *Science, 218,* 1243-1244.

Graf, P., Squire, L. R., & Mandler, G. (1984). The information that amnesic patients do not forget. *Journal of Experimental Psychology: Learning, Memory, and Cognition, 10,* 164-178.

Gray, J. A. (1971). The mind-brain identity theory as a scientific hypothesis. *Philosophical Quarterly, 21,* 247-252.

Gregory, R. L. (1981). *Mind in science.* New York: Cambridge University Press.

Griffin, D. R. (1984). Animal thinking. *American Scientist, 72,* 456-464.

Hamilton, W. (1859). *Lectures on metaphysics and logic* (Vol. 1). Edinburgh: Blackwood.

Harnad, S. (1982). Consciousness: An afterthought. *Cognition and Brain Theory, 5,* 29-47.

Hasher, L., & Zacks, R. T. (1979). Automatic and effortful processes in memory. *Journal of Experimental Psychology: General, 108,* 356-388.

Hebb, D. O. (1949). *The organization of behavior.* New York: Wiley.

Hinton, G. E., & Anderson, J. A. (Eds.) (1981). *Parallel models of associative memory.* Hillsdale, NJ: Lawrence Erlbaum Associates.

Hochberg, J. (1968). In the mind's eye. In R. N. Haber (Ed.), *Contemporary theory and research in visual perception.* New York: Holt.

Hochberg, J. (1981). On cognition in perception: Perceptual coupling and unconscious inference. *Cognition, 10,* 127-134.

Horowitz, L. M., & Prytulak, L. S. (1969). Redintegrative memory. *Psychological Review, 76,* 519-531.

Horton, D. L., & Mills, C. B. (1984). Human learning and memory. In M. R. Rosenzweig & L. W. Porter (Eds.), *Annual Review of Psychology* (Vol. 35). Palo Alto, CA: Annual Reviews.

Hovland, C. I. (1952). A "Communication Analysis" of concept learning. *Psychological Review, 59,* 461-472.

Hull, C. L. (1951). *Essentials of behavior.* New Haven: Yale University Press.

Isen, A. M., & Means, B. (1983). Positive affect as a variable in decision making. *Social Cognition, 2,* 18-31.

Isen, A. M., Means, B., Patrick, R., & Nowicki, G. (1982). Some factors influencing decision-making strategy and risk taking. In M. S. Clark & S. T. Fiske (Eds.), *Affect and cognition: The 17th Annual Carnegie Symposium on Cognition.* Hillsdale, NJ: Lawrence Erlbaum Associates.

Isen, A. M., Shalker, T., Clark, M., & Karp, L. (1978). Affect, accessibility of material in memory and behavior: A cognitive loop?. *Journal of Personality and Social Psychology, 36,* 1-12.

Izard, C. E. (1971). *The face of emotion.* New York: Appleton-Century-Crofts.

Izard, C. E. (1977). *Human emotions.* New York: Plenum Press.

Jacoby, L. L. (1983). Perceptual enhancement: Persistent effects of an experience. *Journal of Experimental Psychology: Learning, Memory, and Cognition, 9,* 21-38.

Jacoby, L. L., & Dallas, M. (1981). On the relationship between autobiographical memory and perceptual learning. *Journal of Experimental Psychology: General, 110,* 306-340.

James, W. (1890). *Principles of psychology.* New York: Holt.

Jenkins, J. J. (Ed.) (1955). *Associative processes in verbal behavior: A report of the Minnesota conference* (Mimeographed report). Department of Psychology, University of Minnesota.

Johnson, M. K., & Raye, C. L. (1981). Reality monitoring. *Psychological Review, 88,* 67-85.

Johnson-Laird, P. (1983). *Mental models.* Cambridge: Cambridge University Press.

Juola, J. F., Fischler, I., Wood, C. T., & Atkinson, R. C. (1971). Recognition time for information stored in long-term memory. *Perception and Psychophysics, 10,* 8-14.

Kahneman, D., & Treisman, A. (1984). Changing views of attention and automaticity. In R. Parasuraman & D. R. Davies (Eds.), *Varieties of attention.* New York: Academic Press.

Kant, I. (1781). *Critique of pure reason* (Translated by N. Kemp Smith). London: Macmillan, 1929.

Katona, G. (1940). *Organizing and memorizing.* New York: Columbia University Press.

Kaufman, E. L., Lord, M. W., Reese, T. W., & Volkmann, J. (1949). The discrimination of visual number. *American Journal of Psychology, 62,* 498-525.

Kessel, F. and Bevan, W. (1985). Notes toward a history of cognitive psychology. In C. W. Buxton (Ed.), *Points of view in the modern history of psychology.* New York: Academic Press.

Kinsbourne, M., & Wood, F. (1982). Theoretical considerations regarding the episodic-semantic memory distinction. In L. S. Cermak (Ed.), *Human memory and amnesia.* Hillsdale, NJ: Lawrence Erlbaum Associates.

Kintsch, W. (1977). Comprehension and memory of text. In W. K. Estes (Ed.), *Handbook of learning and cognitive processes* (Vol. 6). Hillsdale, NJ: Lawrence Erlbaum Associates.

Klapp, S. T., Marshburn, E. A., & Lester, P. T. (1983). Short-term memory does not involve the "working memory" of information processing: The demise of a common assumption. *Journal of Experimental Psychology: General, 112,* 240-264.

Klix, F., & Hoffmann, J. (Eds.) (1980). *Cognition and memory*. Berlin: VEB Deutscher Verlag der Wissenschaften.

Köhler, W. (1929). *Gestalt psychology*. New York: Liveright.

Koffka, K. (1935). *Principles of Gestalt psychology*. New York: Harcourt.

Kosslyn, S. M. (1980). *Image and mind*. Cambridge, Mass.: Harvard University Press.

Kosslyn, S. M. (1983). *Ghosts in the mind's machine*. New York: Norton.

LaBerge, D. (1983). Spatial extent of attention to letters and words. *Journal of Experimental Psychology: Human Perception and Performance, 9*, 371-379.

Lashley, K. S. (1923). The behavioristic interpretation of consciousness. *Psychological Review, 30*, 237-272, 329-353.

Lashley, K. S. (1951). The problem of serial order in behavior. In L. A. Jeffres (Ed.), *Cerebral mechanisms in behavior*. New York: Wiley.

Lazarus, R. S. (1981). A cognitivist's reply to Zajonc on emotion and cognition. *American Psychologist, 36*, 222-223.

Lazarus, R. S. (1984). On the primacy of cognition. *American Psychologist, 39*, 124-129.

Lazarus, R. S., Kanner, A. D., & Folkman, S. (1980). Emotions: A cognitive-phenomenological analysis. In R. Plutchik & H. Kellerman (Eds.), *Theories of emotion*. New York: Academic Press.

Lecocq, P., & Tiberghien, G. (1981). *Mémoire et décision*. Lille: Presses Universitaires de Lille.

Le Ny, J.-F. (1979). *La sémantique psychologique*. Paris: Presses Universitaires de France.

Lounsbury, F. G. (1956). A semantic analysis of the Pawnee kinship usage. *Language, 32*, 158-194.

Macnamara, J. (1972). Cognitive basis of language learning in infants. *Psychological Review, 79*, 1-13.

Mandler, G. (1967a). Organization and memory. In K. W. Spence & J. T. Spence (Eds.), *The psychology of learning and motivation: Advances in research and theory* (Vol. I). New York: Academic Press.

Mandler, G. (1967b). Verbal learning. In G. Mandler, P. Mussen, N. Kogan, & M. A. Wallach (Eds.), *New directions in psychology: III*. New York: Holt, Rinehart, and Winston.

Mandler, G. (1969). Acceptance of things past and present: A look at the mind and the brain. In R. B. McLeod (Ed.), *William James: Unfinished business*. Washington, D.C.: American Psychological Association.

Mandler, G. (1975a). Consciousness: Respectable, useful, and probably necessary. In R. Solso (Ed.), *Information processing and cognition: The Loyola symposium*. Hillsdale, NJ: Lawrence Erlbaum Associates.

Mandler, G. (1975b). Memory storage and retrieval: Some limits on the reach of attention and consciousness. In P. M. A. Rabbitt & S. Dornic (Eds.), *Attention and performance V*. London: Academic Press.

Mandler, G. (1975c). *Mind and emotion*. New York: Wiley.

Mandler, G. (1979a). Organization and repetition: Organizational principles with special reference to rote learning. In L.-G. Nilsson (Ed.), *Perspectives on memory research*. Hillsdale, NJ: Lawrence Erlbaum Associates.

Mandler, G. (1979b). Thought processes, consciousness, and stress. In V. Hamilton & D. M. Warburton (Eds.), *Human stress and cognition: An information processing approach*. London: Wiley.

Mandler, G. (1979c). Organization, memory, and mental structures. In C. R. Puff (Ed.), *Memory organization and structure*. New York: Academic Press.

Mandler, G. (1980). Recognizing: The judgment of previous occurrence. *Psychological Review, 87*, 252-271.

Mandler, G. (1981a). The recognition of previous encounters. *American Scientist, 69*, 211-218.

Mandler, G. (1981b). *What is cognitive psychology? What isn't?* Invited address to the Division of Philosophical Psychology, American Psychological Association, Los Angeles.

Mandler, G. (1982). The integration and elaboration of memory structures. In F. Klix, J. Hoffmann & E. van der Meer (Eds.), *Cognitive research in psychology*. Amsterdam: North Holland.

Mandler, G. (1983). *Consciousness: Its function and construction* (Technical Report No. 117). San Diego: Center for Human Information Processing, University of California.

Mandler, G. (1984a). Cohabitation in the cognitive sciences. In W. Kintsch, J. R. Miller, & P. G. Polson (Eds.), *Method and tactics in cognitive science*. Hillsdale, NJ: Lawrence Erlbaum Associates.

Mandler, G. (1984b). *Mind and body: Psychology of emotion and stress*. New York: Norton.

Mandler, G. (1984c). The construction and limitation of consciousness. In V. Sarris & A. Parducci (Eds.), *Perspectives in psychological experimentation: Toward the year 2000*. Hillside, NJ: Lawrence Erlbaum Associates.

Mandler, G. (1985). From association to structure. *Journal of Experimental Psychology: Learning, Memory, and Cognition*, in press.

Mandler, G., & Graesser, A. C. II (1975). Dimensional analysis and the locus of organization. Technical Report No.48, San Diego: Center for Human Information Processing, University of California. Published as: Analyse dimensionelle et le "locus" de l'organisation. In S. Ehrlich & E. Tulving (Eds.), *La mémoire sémantique*. Paris: Bulletin de Psychologie, 1976.

Mandler, G., & Huttenlocher, J. (1956). The relationship between associative frequency, associative ability and paired-associate learning. *American Journal of Psychology*, *69*, 424-428.

Mandler, G., & Kessen, W. (1959). *The language of psychology*. New York: Wiley.

Mandler, G., & Kessen, W. (1974). The appearance of free will. In S. C. Brown (Ed.), *Philosophy of psychology*. London: Macmillan.

Mandler, G., & Kuhlman, C. K. (1961). Proactive and retroactive effects of overlearning. *Journal of Experimental Psychology*, *61*, 76-81.

Mandler, G., Pearlstone, Z., & Koopmans, H. J. (1969). Effects of organization and semantic similarity on recall and recognition. *Journal of Verbal Learning and Verbal Behavior*, *8*, 410-423.

Mandler, G., & Shebo, B. J. (1982). Subitizing: An analysis of its component processes. *Journal of Experimental Psychology: General*, *111*, 1-22.

Mandler, G., & Shebo, B. J. (1983). Knowing and liking. *Motivation and Emotion*, *7*, 125-144.

Mandler, J. M. (1983). Representation. In J. H. Flavell & E. M. Markham (Eds.), *Cognitive development*. Vol. 3 of P. Mussen (Ed.), *Handbook of child psychology*. New York: Wiley.

Mandler, J. M. (1984a). Representation and recall in infancy. In M. Moscovitch (Ed.), *Infant memory*. New York: Plenum.

Mandler, J. M. (1984b). *Stories, scripts, and scenes: Aspects of schema theory*. Hillsdale, NJ: Lawrence Erlbaum Associates.

Mandler, J. M., & Mandler, G. (1964). *Thinking: From Association to Gestalt*. New York: Wiley (Reprint edition: Westport, Conn.: Greenwood Press, 1981).

Mandler, J. M., & Mandler, G. (1974). Good guys vs. bad guys: The subject-object dichotomy. *Journal of Humanistic Psychology*, *14*, 63-87.

Marcel, A. J. (1983a). Conscious and unconscious perception: Experiments on visual masking and word recognition. *Cognitive Psychology*, *15*, 197-237.

Marcel, A. J. (1983b). Conscious and unconscious perception: An approach to the relations between phenomenal experience and perceptual processes. *Cognitive Psychology*, *15*, 238-300.

McClelland, J. L. (1979). On the time relations of mental processes: An examination of systems of processes in cascade. *Psychological Review*, *86*, 287-330.

McClelland, J. L., & Rumelhart, D. E. (1981). An interactive activation model of context effects in letter perception: Part 1. An account of basic findings. *Psychological Review*, *88*, 375-407.

McClelland, J. L. & Rumelhart, D. E. (1985). *Parallel distributed processing: Explorations on the microstructure of cognition* (Vol. 2 - Applications). Cambridge, MA: MIT Press.

McCloskey, M., & Santee, J. (1981). Are semantic memory and episodic memory distinct systems? *Journal of Experimental Psychology: Human Learning and Memory*, *7*, 66-71.

McCorduck, P. (1979). *Machines who think*. San Francisco: W. H. Freeman & Co.

McKoon, G., & Ratcliff, R. (1979). Priming in episodic and semantic memory. *Journal of Verbal Learning and Verbal Behavior*, *18*, 463-480.

Mechanisation of thought processes. (1959). (Symposium No. 10, National Physical Laboratory). London: Her Majesty's Stationery Office.

Melzack, R. (1973). *The puzzle of pain*. New York: Basic Books.

Merzenich, M. M., Nelson, R. J., Stryker, M. P., Cynader, M. S., Schoppmann, A., & Zook, J. M. (1984). Somatosensory cortical map changes following digit amputation in adult monkeys. *Journal of Comparative Neurology*, *224*, 591-605.

Meyer, D. E., & Schvaneveldt, R. W. (1976). Meaning, memory structure, and mental process. In C. N. Cofer (Ed.), *The structure of human memory*. San Francisco: Freeman.

Miller, G. A. (1956). The magical number seven, plus or minus two: Some limits on our capacity for processing information. *Psychological Review*, *63*, 81-97.

Miller, G. A. (1962). *Psychology: The science of mental life*. New York: Harper & Row.

Miller, G. A. (1979). *A very personal history* (Occasional paper No. 1). Center for Cognitive Sciences, Massachusetts Institute of Technology.

Miller, G. A., Galanter, E. H., & Pribram, K. (1960). *Plans and the structure of behavior*. New York: Holt.

Minsky, M. (1975). A framework for representing knowledge. In P. H. Winston (Ed.), *The psychology of computer vision*. New York: McGraw-Hill.

Mischel, W. (1968). *Personality and assessment*. New York: Wiley.

Morton, J. (1969). Interaction of information in word recognition. *Psychological Review*, *76*, 165-178.

Muenzinger, K. F. (1938). Vicarious trial and error at a point of choice. I. A general survey of its relation to learning efficiency. *Journal of Genetic Psychology, 53,* 75-86.

Natsoulas, T. (1970). Concerning introspective "knowledge". *Psychological Bulletin, 73,* 89-111.

Natsoulas, T. (1977). Consciousness: Consideration of an inferential hypothesis. *Journal for the Theory of Social Behavior, 7,* 29-39.

Neisser, U. (1967). *Cognitive psychology.* New York: Appleton-Century-Crofts.

Newell, A. (1973). Production systems: Models of control structure. In W. Chase (Ed.), *Visual information processing.* New York: Academic Press.

Newell, A., & Simon, H. (1972). *Human problem solving.* Englewood Cliffs, NJ: Prentice-Hall.

Nisbett, R. E., & Wilson, T. D. (1977). Telling more than we can know: Verbal reports on mental processes. *Psychological Review, 84,* 231-259.

Norman, D. A. (1980). Twelve issues for cognitive science. *Cognitive Science, 4,* 1-32.

Norman, D. A. (1982). Some observations on mental models. In D. Gentner & A. Stevens (Eds.), *Mental models.* Hillsdale, NJ: Lawrence Erlbaum Associates.

Norman, D. A., & Bobrow, D. G. (1979). Descriptions: An intermediate stage in memory retrieval. *Cognitive Psychology, 11,* 107-123.

Norman, D. A., & Rumelhart, D. E. (1975). *Explorations in cognition.* San Francisco: Freeman.

Norman, D. A., & Shallice, T. (1980). *Attention to action: Willed and automatic control of behavior* (Technical Report No. 99). San Diego: Center for Human Information Processing, University of California.

Obrist, P. A., Sutterer, J. R., & Howard, J. L. (1972). Preparatory cardiac changes: A psychobiological approach. In A. H. Black & W. F. Prokasy (Eds.), *Classical conditioning II.* New York: Appleton-Century-Crofts.

Ortony, A., Collins, A., & Clore, G. L. (1982). *Principia pathematica.* Unpublished manuscript.

Palmer, S. E. (1978). Fundamental aspects of cognitive representation. In E. Rosch & B. B. Lloyd (Eds.), *Cognition and categorization.* Hillsdale, NJ: Lawrence Erlbaum Associates.

Piaget, J. (1953). *The origin of intelligence in the child.* London: Routledge & Kegan Paul.

Piaget, J. (1970). Piaget's theory. In P. Mussen (Ed.), *Carmichael's manual of child psychology* (Vol. 1) Third edition. New York: Wiley.

Posner, M. I. (1969). Abstraction and the process of recognition. In J. T. Spence & G. H. Bower (Eds.), *Advances in learning and motivation* (Vol. 3). New York: Academic Press.

Posner, M. I., & Boies, S. J. (1971). Components of attention. *Psychological Review, 78*, 391-408.

Posner, M. I., & Snyder, C. R. R. (1975). Attention and cognitive control. In R. Solso (Ed.), *Information processing and cognition: The Loyola symposium.* Potomac, Md.: Lawrence Erlbaum Associates.

Postman, L., Bruner, J. S., & McGinnies, E. (1948). Personal values as selective factors in perception. *Journal of Abnormal and Social Psychology, 43*, 142-154.

Reisberg, D., Rappaport, I., & O'Shaughnessy, M. (1984). Limits of working memory: The digit digit-span. *Journal of Experimental Psychology: Learning, Memory, and Cognition, 10*, 203-221.

Rescorla, R. A. (1967). Pavlovian conditioning and its proper control procedures. *Psychological Review, 74*, 71-80.

Restle, F. (1970). Theory of serial pattern learning: Structural trees. *Psychological Review, 77*, 481-495.

Révész, G. (Ed.) (1954). *Thinking and speaking: A symposium.* Amsterdam: North Holland Publishing Company.

Rock, I. (1957). The role of repetition in associative learning. *American Journal of Psychology, 70*, 186-193.

Rosch, E. (1978). Principles of categorization. In E. Rosch & B. B. Lloyd (Eds.), *Cognition and categorization.* Hillsdale, NJ: Lawrence Erlbaum Associates.

Rosch, E., & Mervis, C. (1975). Family resemblances: Studies in the internal structure of categories. *Cognitive Psychology, 7*, 573-605.

Ross, B. H. (1984). Remindings and their effects in learning a cognitive skill. *Cognitive Psychology, 16*, 371-416.

Rumelhart, D.E., & McClelland, J.L. (1982). An interactive activation model of context effects in letter perception: Part 2. The contextual enhancement effect and some tests and extensions of the model. *Psychological Review, 89*, 60-94.

Rumelhart, D. E. & McClelland, J. L. (1985). *Parallel distributed processing: Explorations on the microstructure of cognition* (Vol. 1 - Foundations). Cambridge, MA: MIT Press.

Rumelhart, D. E., & Norman, D. A. (in press). Representation in memory. In R. C. Atkinson, R. J. Herrnstein, G. Lindzey & R. D. Luce (Eds.), *Handbook of experimental psychology.* New York: Wiley.

Rumelhart, D. E., & Ortony, A. (1978). The representation of knowledge in memory. In R. C. Anderson, R. J. Spiro, & W. E. Montague (Eds.), *Schooling and the acquisition of knowledge.* Hillsdale, NJ: Lawrence Erlbaum Associates.

Sakitt, B. (1976). Iconic memory. *Psychological Review, 83*, 257-276.

Schachter, S., & Singer, J. E. (1962). Cognitive, social and physiological determinants of emotional state. *Psychological Review, 69,* 379-399.

Schank, R., & Abelson, R. (1977). *Scripts, plans, goals and understanding: An inquiry into human knowledge structures.* Hillsdale, NJ: Lawrence Erlbaum Associates.

Schneiderman, S. (1983). *Jacques Lacan: The death of an intellectual hero.* Cambridge, MA: Harvard University Press.

Selfridge, O. (1959). Pandemonium: A paradigm for learning. In *Mechanisation of thought processes* (Vol. 1). London: Her Majesty's Stationery Office.

Selz, O. (1913). *Ueber die Gesetze des geordneten Denkverlaufs. Eine experimentelle Untersuchung.* Stuttgart: Spemann.

Shallice, T. (1972). Dual functions of consciousness. *Psychological Review, 79,* 383-393.

Shanon, B. (1983). *Thought sequences.* Working paper No. 5, Department of Psychology, The Hebrew University of Jerusalem.

Shepard, R. N. (1978). The mental image. *American Psychologist, 33,* 125-137.

Shepard, R. N., & Metzler, J. (1971). Mental rotation of three-dimensional objects. *Science, 171,* 701-703.

Shiffrin, R. M., & Schneider, W. (1977). Controlled and automatic human information processing: II. Perceptual learning, automatic attending, and a general theory. *Psychological Review, 84,* 127-190.

Skinner, B. F. (1964). Behaviorism at fifty. In T. W. Wann (Ed.), *Behaviorism and phenomenology.* Chicago: University of Chicago Press.

Snygg, D., & Combs, A. W. (1949). *Individual behavior.* New York: Harper.

Sperling, G. (1960). The information available in brief visual presentations. *Psychological Monographs, 74 (Whole No. 498).*

Sternberg, S. (1966). High-speed scanning in human memory. *Science, 153,* 652-654.

Sulloway, F. J. (1979). *Freud, biologist of the mind: Beyond the psychoanalytic legend.* New York: Basic Books.

Thatcher, R. W., & John, E. R. (1977). *Foundations of cognitive processes.* Hillsdale, NJ: Lawrence Erlbaum Associates.

Titchener, E. B. (1898). Postulates of a structural psychology. *Philosophical Review, 7,* 449-465.

Tomkins, S. S. (1981). The quest for primary motives: Biography and autobiography of an idea. *Journal of Personality and Social Psychology, 41,* 306-329.

Treisman, A. M. (1964). Verbal cues, language and meaning in selective attention. *American Journal of Psychology, 77,* 206-218.

Treisman, A. (1969). Strategies and models of selective attention. *Psychological Review*, *76*, 282-299.

Treisman, A. M., & Gelade, G. (1980). A feature-integration theory of attention. *Cognitive Psychology*, *12*, 97-136.

Tulving, E. (1983). *Elements of episodic memory*. Oxford: Oxford University Press.

Tulving, E., Schacter, D. L., & Stark, H. A. (1982). Priming effects in word-fragment completion are independent of recognition memory. *Journal of Experimental Psychology: Learning, Memory, and Cognition*, *8*, 336-342.

Tulving, E., & Thomson, D. M. (1973). Encoding specificity and retrieval processes in episodic memory. *Psychological Review*, *80*, 352-373.

Turvey, M. T. (1977). Contrasting orientations to the theory of visual information processing. *Psychological Review*, *84*, 67-88.

Tversky, A., & Kahneman, D. (1973). Availability: A heuristic for judging frequency and probability. *Cognitive Psychology*, *5*, 207-232.

Vygotsky, L. S. (1962). *Thought and language*. Cambridge, MA: M. I. T. Press.

Warrington, E. K. (1975). The selective impairment of semantic memory. *Quarterly Journal of Experimental Psychology*, *27*, 635-657.

Warrington, E. K., & Weiskrantz, L. (1970). Amnesia: Consolidation or retrieval? *Nature*, *228*, 628-630.

Warrington, E. K., & Weiskrantz, L. (1974). The effect of prior learning on subsequent retention in amnesic patients. *Neuropsychologia*, *12*, 419-428.

Warrington, E. K., & Weiskrantz, L. (1982). Amnesia: A disconnection syndrome? *Neuropsychologia*, *20*, 233-248.

Waugh, N. C., & Norman, D. A. (1965). Primary memory. *Psychological Review*, *72*, 89-104.

Wickelgren, W. A. (1979). Chunking consolidation: A theoretical synthesis of semantic networks, configuring in conditioning, S-R vs. cognitive learning, normal forgetting, the amnesic syndrome and the hippocampal arousal system. *Psychological Review*, *86*, 44-60.

Wittgenstein, L. (1953). *Philosophical investigations* (Translated by G. E. M. Anscombe). New York: Macmillan, 1963.

Woolsey, C. N. (Ed.) (1981-1982). *Cortical sensory organization* (Vols. 1-3). Clifton, NJ: Humana Press.

Zajonc, R. B. (1980). Feeling and thinking: Preferences need no inferences. *American Psychologist*, *35*, 151-175.

Zajonc, R. B. (1984). On the primacy of affect. *American Psychologist*, *39*, 117-123.

Zborowski, M. (1969). *People in pain*. San Francisco: Jossey-Bass.

Name Index

Subject Index